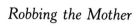

Robbing the Mother

Robbing the Mother

Women in Faulkner

DEBORAH CLARKE

University Press of Mississippi
Jackson

Copyright © 1994 by University Press of Mississippi
Manufactured in the United States of America

97 96 95 94   4 3 2 1

The paper in this book meets the guidelines for permanence and durability of the
Committee on Production Guidelines for Book Longevity of the Council on Library
Resources.

Library of Congress Cataloging-in-Publication Data

Clarke, Deborah, 1956–
    Robbing the mother : women in Faulkner / Deborah Clarke.
        p.   cm.
    Includes bibliographical references and index.
    ISBN 0-87805-592-4 (alk. paper)
        1. Faulkner, William, 1897–1962—Characters—Women.   2. Women and
literature—United States—History—20th century.   3. Motherhood—In
literature.   4. Mothers—In literature.   5. Women—In literature.   I. Title.
PS3511.A86Z7547   1994
813'.52—dc20   93-33642
                                                                                CIP

British Library Cataloging-in-Publication data available

For

MY PARENTS

Contents

Acknowledgments

This book draws on so many fine studies of Faulkner that I cannot hope to place it in relation to all of them. A few, however, stand out as especially influential. John Irwin's pathbreaking *Doubling and Incest / Repetition and Revenge* helped to illuminate psychological issues in Faulkner's work, suggesting ways of reconceptualizing those concerns from the mother's perspective. Eric Sundquist's examination of race in *The House Divided* offered an exceedingly useful model for recognizing the significance of difference in Faulkner's artistic vision. John Matthews's work on language in Faulkner has contributed to my understanding of how Faulkner presents language as gendered, growing out of absent referents. Minrose Gwin's *The Feminine and Faulkner,* which appeared while this project was nearing completion, provided an extremely useful feminist model and helped me to sharpen my focus and pursue the implications of my arguments. While Gwin and I clearly employ some similar theoretical perspectives, my treatment looks less at sexual difference than at gendered language, less at bisexuality than at maternity. I am also indebted to Doreen Fowler and Carolyn Porter, both for their encouragement and for their work, which provided further confirmation of the value of applying feminist psychoanalytic theory to Faulkner.

In addition, many people have offered valuable advice and support at all stages of this project. In particular, I thank Seetha A-Srinivasan at the University Press of Mississippi for her great patience with a book that was always behind schedule and for her belief in the project itself. Lyall Powers first introduced me to Faulkner's work, and R. W. B. Lewis supervised the dissertation out of which evolved the first seeds of this project. I thank Sue Schweik, Ruth Hoberman, and Beth Kalikoff, who read early stages of the project with great care and provided me with a strong framework for piecing everything together. Two research assistants—Joan Sebastian at Eastern Illinois University and James Hurley at Penn State University— did excellent work helping me to track down and evaluate the vast body of relevant Faulkner criticism. I also thank my Penn State students, particularly those in my Faulkner seminars, for listening, responding, and significantly contributing to my greater understanding of what I was trying to say. Rosa Eberly read large chunks of the manuscript and offered much-needed advice and reassurance. I am also grateful to Susan Harris for her valuable help with last-minute fine-tuning. My officemate, Laura Knoppers, has endured my anxieties, my complaints, and my appropriation of the office computer with good will and compassion. Finally, to many other friends and colleagues too numerous to name, and to my family, I give thanks for advice, support, encouragement, and friendship.

Research for this project was partially funded by a National Endowment for the Humanities summer stipend. An early version of the *Sound and the Fury* section of Chapter 2 was presented at the 1991 Faulkner and Yoknapatawpha Conference at the University of Mississippi. An early version of the *Light in August* section of Chapter 4 was published as "Gender, Race, and Language in *Light in August*," *American Literature* 61 (October 1989): 398–413. Chapter 5 is a greatly revised and expanded version of "Familiar and Fantastic: Women in *Absalom, Absalom!*" *Faulkner Journal* 2 (Fall 1986): 62–72.

Abbreviations and Texts

References are to the following editions of Faulkner's novels:

AA   *Absalom, Absalom!* (1936). Vintage, 1987.
AILD   *As I Lay Dying* (1930). Vintage, 1987.
Ham   *The Hamlet* (1931). Vintage, 1956.
LA   *Light in August* (1932). Vintage International, 1990.
OS   *Sanctuary: The Original Text.* Ed. Noel Polk. Random House, 1990.
San   *Sanctuary* (1931). Vintage, 1987.
SF   *The Sound and the Fury* (1929). Vintage, 1987.
WP   *The Wild Palms* (1939). Vintage, 1939.

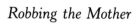

Robbing the Mother

Chapter 1

"Worth Any Number of Old Ladies"

If a writer has to rob his mother, he will not hesitate;
the "Ode on a Grecian Urn" is worth any number
of old ladies.
Faulkner, *Lion in the Garden*

Coming from a man so devoted to his mother that he apparently visited her every day he spent in Oxford, this cavalier treatment of the mother's claims sounds suspiciously like the tongue-in-cheek statements so common in Faulkner's interviews. Humorously intended or not, Faulkner's remark about the devotion of a writer to "his" work also encapsulates many of his contradictory feelings about a figure he generally associates with creativity: woman. Much literary theory defines the process of writing as a kind of patricide—responding to and often silencing one's precursor/father figures. Faulkner, however, also identifies women as part of the struggle for literary creativity. If one has to outdo one's father, one also must essentially undo one's mother, whom Faulkner casts not as an opponent but as a source. Still, she too must die, or at least disappear. What she has, what she embodies, must be appropriated by any possible means; the writer lives off—and ultimately kills off—"his" mother, as the initial robbery rapidly becomes a murder, with the poem's "worth" displacing and replacing that of the women. The "Ode on a Grecian Urn" is "worth any number of old ladies" because those old ladies somehow originate the artistic vision; without them there can be no sustenance and hence, no art. Even then, the art cannot be manifested until it has been wrested from them.

Faulkner's choice of the "Grecian Urn" as a literary achievement for which many old women could justly be sacrificed is particularly interesting, for what the poem says about women precisely describes the feelings of many of his male characters. Keats's poetic vision is founded upon a "still unravish'd bride of quietness," implying that art grows out of women's sexual innocence, passivity, and silence. The male "Bold lover" at least will love forever; the silent female object will be forever "fair." The poem appears repeatedly in his novels, almost always in relation to women. Horace Benbow of *Flags in the Dust* refers to his sister Narcissa as "thou still unravished bride of quietude" (398); Lena Grove's journey in *Light in August* is described as "something moving forever and without progress across an urn" (7). Later in the same novel, however, when Bobbie Allan tells Joe Christmas about menstruation, signal of woman's ability to become a mother, Joe "seemed to see a diminishing row of suavely shaped urns in moonlight, blanched. And not one was perfect. Each one was cracked and from each crack there issued something liquid, deathcolored, and foul" (189). If woman is represented by the "suavely shaped" urns, this imagery, suggests Gail Mortimer, evokes "both the smooth, alluring surface of the beautiful object and the awareness that a somehow threatening reality lies beneath" ("Smooth" 150). That "reality" reminds us that women's creativity is signaled by the presence of "deathcolored and foul" blood, by reminders of the dominance of the body itself. The potential for physical maternity cracks the artistic vessel of femininity, violating the unravished bride.

Thus, while the "Grecian Urn" may be worth many mothers, it also retains the physical traces of their bodies, as Faulkner documents the urn's failure to contain the maternal creativity it has usurped. This maternal creativity has many implications, both life-threatening and life-affirming. Since the pregnant Lena evokes the urn with a sense of peace and serenity, it appears that motherhood itself may not be the force which cracks the urn. It is the menstrual blood, the corporeal evidence of women's physical procreative power, which reveals the threatening interior. Even though Joe Christmas views menstrual blood as a desecration of women, reducing them to "victims of periodical filth" (*LA* 185), Faulkner uses this desecration to investigate the full extent of what female creativity entails. Philip

Weinstein suggests that for Faulkner maternity is "a sort of narrative Waterloo: an incoherent zone his fiction can lead up to and away from but which none of his women can traverse and still remain themselves" (12). This depends on how one defines the self; certainly maternity has a profound impact on women's identity, but it does not constitute the ultimate defeat which Weinstein envisions. Rather, it opens up an exhilarating and frightening creative potential, as both men and women must confront the transformative power of the mother.

This power, despite the occasional idealization of motherhood, is grounded in the literal. The bloody functioning of female sexual organs reveals the reality behind the ideal, that the physical, not the linguistic, provides the engendering power, a power which grows out of female sexuality. Without "filth," there would be no creation, as the womb both nourishes and threatens life, reminding men of their origins and their dependence on women's bodies for their very existences. Faulkner's most interesting women—Caddy Compson, Addie Bundren, Dewey Dell Bundren, Temple Drake, Eula Varner, Lena Grove, Joanna Burden, Charlotte Rittenmeyer, Rosa Coldfield—are rarely unravished and rarely passive. They have bodies which often prove uncontainable by a phallogocentric society. Their maternal power, whether presented literally or figuratively, grants them an artistic counterforce to the linguistically constructed urn.

The poetic urn, a figurative creation of linguistic artistry, is thus displaced by a physical female body with all its bodily excretions, setting up a tension between figurative and literal, language and maternity. "If language, like culture, sets up a separation and, starting with discrete elements, concatenates an order," says Julia Kristeva, "it does so precisely by repressing maternal authority and the corporeal mapping that abuts against them" (*Horror* 72). In Faulkner's work, maternal authority, especially when aligned with the corporeal body, challenges the dominance of language. Kristeva goes on to question what happens "when the legal, phallic, linguistic symbolic establishment does not carry out the separation in radical fashion." What happens is that Addie Bundren realizes that words are no good, that Quentin Compson must kill himself rather than face a sister's physical maternity, that Rosa Coldfield erupts into the center of *Absalom, Absalom!* and throws the narrative and genealogical line into complete disarray. When the "phallic, linguistic symbolic establishment" fails to suppress maternal authority, it reveals the precariousness of its own power and definition.

Into this dearth of phallogocentric control comes the disruptive presence of women, with the potential to redefine established conventions and to suggest different methods of creativity. Thus Faulkner, who may very well have feared and distrusted women, also sees in them a mysterious, often threatening power, which is aligned with his own creativity and the grounds of his own fiction. Seldom has a writer examined so thoroughly and so obsessively the concept of woman as other. Yet ultimately the boundaries of that "otherness" break down, and women become uncannily and paradoxically the emblems of his fictional vision. When we examine Faulkner's women and other characters' responses to them, we find that they often mirror the tensions and ambivalences of Faulkner's artistic style in ways which men do not. For Hélène Cixous, "Woman un-thinks the unifying, regulating history that homogenizes and channels forces, herding contradictions into a single battlefield" (252). Because Faulkner sets himself against history as a unifying and homogenizing force, essentially a masculine ideal, women provide him with the undoing factor he needs to fight the concept, particularly in *Absalom, Absalom!,* where Miss Rosa rewrites patriarchal history in "notlanguage."

Clearly, not all of Faulkner's women evoke the power of a Rosa Coldfield or an Addie Bundren, but his greatest novels often rely on the presence of disruptive femininity. In fact, one could argue that the only women presented as non-threatening are the old ladies, those no longer sexually active. Miss Jenny DuPre of *Flags* and Granny Millard in *The Unvanquished* are asexual matriarchs who fight to preserve the patriarchy, old ladies who might willingly offer their lives for the "Grecian Urn." Upholding the glory of the Old South, they have little control over the new order. Yet even Granny Millard intrudes into male territory as she proves a greater threat to the Yankees than either Colonel Sartoris or General Forrest. And the limited refuge the old ladies provide breaks down completely when we consider Rosa Coldfield or Emily Grierson. Not even age and menopause necessarily render women less threatening; the only safe woman is a dead woman, until Addie Bundren speaks from her coffin.

Another argument finds Faulkner's strong women to be honorary men—Joanna Burden and Charlotte Rittenmeyer, for example. But reading them as masculine misrepresents Faulkner's construction of gender and fails to account for the equivalent strength residing with such "real women" as Lena Grove and the pregnant woman of *The Wild Palms,* who turn out to be not so different from their less "feminine" counterparts.

Karen Ramsay Johnson notes that to achieve artistic creation in Faulkner's work, "the traditional male and female sex roles must be confused and conflated as the writer (and reader) rejects stable categories of self-definition to participate in the re-creative process of narration" (1). To define Faulkner's women by classification, then, and to miss the creative potential in the collapse of conventional gender boundaries is to commit the same acts of misreading into which his male characters invariably fall. Even within their female roles, his women defy categorization. Eula Varner, for example, becomes both virginity and fertility embodied, while Caddy Compson functions as sister, mother, and whore. Women's fluid and contradictory identities challenge the labeling by which such men as Mr. Compson—as well as many readers and critics—attempt to define them. Feminist theory provides alternative approaches which can open up new avenues into Faulkner's work, revealing his recognition that gender is not necessarily fixed, and does not always conform to expected patriarchal norms. Most importantly, feminist theory offers a framework to examine maternal power and to understand that the mother has as much, if not more, to do with identity, order, and language as the father.

Coppélia Kahn, writing on *King Lear,* notes that "patriarchal structures loom obviously on the surface of many texts, structures of authority, control, force, logic, linearity, misogyny, male superiority. But beneath them, as in a palimpsest, we can find what I call 'the maternal subtext,' the imprint of mothering on the male psyche, the psychological presence of the mother whether or not mothers are literally represented as characters" (35). This "psychological presence of the mother" resonates throughout Faulkner's work as a locus of creative power, a presence to be reckoned with by any possible means. Robbing the mother becomes Faulkner's "maternal subtext," as he reveals both the imprint of mothering and the voiding of it, trading in his mother for the "Ode on a Grecian Urn." This exchange of mother for poetry suggests a movement from body to language, literal to figurative, semiotic to symbolic, feminine to masculine. Yet robbing the mother also positions her as a source, thus granting her a certain power to generate poetic language. And who's to say whether she might not try to recapture her purloined letters? Thus women in Faulkner's fiction become both the source of and the threat to figurative creativity.

It can be difficult to pinpoint the exact nature of the maternal threat, for on the surface, many of Faulkner's women appear shallow, mindless, and even perverted. Often, they have little to say for themselves. But beneath that silence lurks a kind of language different from that of standard symbolic discourse. Clytie, for example, reveals the Sutpen secret not through words but through the text of her interracial body. Writing of her southern heritage and upbringing, Shirley Abbott, in *Womenfolks,* sheds light on the position of women in the South of Faulkner's time: "I grew up believing, though I could never have voiced it, that a woman might pose as garrulous and talky and silly and dotty, but at heart she was a steely, silent creature, with secrets no man could ever know, and she was always—always— stronger than any man" (3). This suggestion that women fabricate an external pose, remaining unable to "voice" their knowledge yet holding "secrets no man could ever know," rings true for many of Faulkner's women. Yet his description of female duality takes on a slightly more sinister tone, illustrated through the suavely shaped urn filled with death-colored liquid. Both Abbott and Faulkner, however, testify to the gap in comprehension and expression between men and women. Her wording recalls *Light in August;* when Byron Bunch hears Lena Grove's moans during childbirth, he feels that she "seemed to be speaking clearly to something in a tongue which he knew was not his tongue nor that of any man" (399).

Women's language—talky yet silent, lucid yet foreign—lies at the core of their mysterious strength. Few writers focus on the problematic nature of language more thoroughly than Faulkner. His compulsively over-articulate male protagonists fling words around like frisbees, constantly seeking to assert mastery through linguistic control. His women, on the other hand, recognize language's limitations. As Margaret Powers puts it in *Soldier's Pay,* "Women know more about words than men ever will. And they know how little they can ever possibly mean" (250). Out-talking women is analogous to the young Thomas Sutpen's realization that killing the "monkey nigger" who turns him away from the front door will do no good because it would be like "hitting a child's toy balloon with a face painted on it, a face slick and smooth and distended and about to burst into laughing and so you did not dare strike it because it would merely burst" (*AA* 287). The "monkey nigger" is just a symbol, so in attacking it one merely challenges the sign rather than the signified. Destroying a slave eradicates neither slavery nor the class hierarchy which supports it. Likewise, out-talking women does not defeat the mother's literal and figurative procreative power. The smooth distended balloon of Sutpen's imagination can be recast as a pregnant woman, a mother-to-be. One cannot defeat it by force, because bursting the pregnant woman delivers the child and thus reaffirms her control over creativity. So, one must attempt to deflate it, to empty it of its substance and thus its significance, to remove it from the realm of the corporeal where the mother reigns.

But why the mother? What is it about motherhood—both literal and figurative—that makes it such a powerful imaginative force? While Fairchild dismisses, in *Mosquitoes,* women's claim to artistic creation through childbirth—"biology takes care of that. . . .But in art, a man can create without any assistance at all" (320)—Faulkner realizes that art and biology can intersect in interesting ways. As Alice Jardine notes,

> Male writers have needed the loving support of their muses, mistresses, or mothers in order then to put them aside, deny them, reject them, idealize them or kill them in their writing, but, in any case, to *ingest* them so as better to evacuate them, purify themselves, and identify with the Father—if only then to kill him like the good sons they are. (89)

Jardine's metaphor of ingested women in some ways better describes the relation between men and women, art and femininity, than robbery, which defines the mother as victim. To ingest the mother, however, is to internalize femininity, something that men in Faulkner's work do at their peril. For Faulkner himself the meal proves more productive, for when he ingests the mother it is not necessarily to "evacuate" her and identify with the father. As a writer, he retains a kind of maternal position, with control over literal and linguistic creativity.

Consequently, the maternal creativity presented in Faulkner's work transcends childbirth. In *Mosquitoes,* the Semitic man lists women's ability to "bear geniuses" as their sole contribution to art, for women care nothing about "the pictures and music their children produce" (248). Mothers in Faulkner's work, however, bear far more than geniuses; indeed, they bear few if any of them. Rather, they bear the origins of language and identity. Because the mother represents both origin and other, self and not-self, as Madelon Sprengnether argues, "she has a ghostlike function, creating a presence out of absence" (5). Creating a presence out of absence exactly describes Caddy's role in *The Sound and the Fury,* but Faulkner extends this premise well beyond the roles of the women. One need only recall the way Quentin and Shreve create a tale out of a ghostly absence in *Absalom* to realize that creating presence out of absence is fundamental to Faulkner's narrative. His fictional enterprise, which so often subverts its own order and authority, can be investigated in terms of its connection to the maternal.

The relationship between maternity and language has received a great deal of attention from feminist critics, who draw on and revise Lacan's Law of the Father, seeking a place for the realm and discourse of the mother. Margaret Homans, in examining the origins of the dominance of cultural discourse, notes that in Western culture, "the death or absence of the mother sorrowfully but fortunately makes possible the construction of language and culture" (2). She cites the *Oresteia,* in which Orestes is acquitted of the charge of matricide because Apollo argues that "The mother is no parent of that which is called her child, but only nurse of the new-planted seed that grows. The parent is he who mounts." The power of the mother must be erased and the Furies—avengers of matricide— silenced in order to found Athenian culture. The mother is displaced by cultural law and cultural language.

This silencing of the mother carries over into the ways language is gendered. Women tend to be relegated to the literal and natural, excluded from the discourses of law, culture, and figurative creativity. As Homans argues, "literal language, together with nature and matter to which it is epistemologically linked, is traditionally classified as feminine, and the feminine is, from the point of view of a predominantly androcentric culture, always elsewhere too" (4). In literary creativity, figurative discourse, of course, is more highly valued and, Homans asserts, "associated with the masculine. To take something literally is to get it wrong, while to have a figurative understanding of something is the correct intellectual stance" (5). She goes on to illustrate how women writers respond to gendered language, noting that they view the literal with ambivalence; it is associated with the feminine, yet represents a lesser form of literary creativity. Faulkner, too, I would argue, shares this ambivalent stance toward the literal which both enables and endangers his fiction. While ostensibly recognizing the gendering of literal and figurative language, he also challenges and collapses their respective valuations and even the division between them.

In further examining and reinforcing the cultural myth of masculine control over feminine language, Jacques Lacan offers his theory of the Law of the Father and relates the acquisition of language to the phallus. Up until about eighteen months of age, he postulates, a child engages in nonverbal communication with the mother, unmediated by formal language. At that point, Lacan suggests, the child begins both to acquire language and to recognize his difference from his mother. Because the earlier communication with the mother has been largley nonverbal, the child associates linguistic conversation with the father, owner of the phallus. Thus symbolic discourse—language—is predicated upon difference from the mother. To enter in to the language of the Father, one leaves behind the unmediated communion with the mother and instead replaces that unity with symbolic figures for her. Of course, it is only boys who can fully integrate this symbolic power, for girls grow up recognizing their exclusion from symbolic discourse and, consequently, develop a more problematic relation to language than boys do.

> There is no woman who is not excluded by the nature of things, which is the nature of words, and it must be said that, if there is something they complain a lot about at the moment, that is what it is—except that they don't know what they are saying, that's the whole difference between them and me. (quoted in Irigaray 87)

Women are excluded in this model because the nature of words defines reality, and words are associated with the father. "There is no prediscursive reality," says Lacan. "Every reality is based upon and defined by a discourse" (quoted in Irigaray 88). "Reality," then, is grounded on separation from and repression of the mother. Feminist revisions of Lacan, however, refocus attention on the notion of the prediscursive reality which he denies, the nonverbal language of the mother. This form of communication is predicated on sameness rather than difference, on literal rather than figurative expression.

The mother may exert considerable control over symbolic discourse as well. While Lacanian paradigms identify the acquisition of language with the father, we grant the mother a greater role in that acquisition if we focus on the birth process rather than the oedipal stage as critical in the development of the individual. If birth represents the primal separation and loss, then the child is impelled back toward the mother rather than into the domain and language of the father, for birth acts as both a break from the mother and a reunion with her. Mary Jacobus asserts that maternity itself can be seen as division, "the process of separation which gives rise both to the subject and to language" (147). The mother becomes the origin of self and language, but it is an origin, particularly in Faulkner's work, which threatens to re-engulf both. As Quentin observes, "the dungeon was Mother herself" (*SF* 198).

Furthermore, language, born of the mother, takes on some of her characteristics. John Matthews points out that Faulkner's language "simultaneously erodes the autonomy and discreteness of selfhood even as it creates them" (16). This simultaneous erosion and creation of self corresponds to the function of the preoedipal mother, which Kristeva links to the preverbal semiotic, "the place where the subject is both generated and negated" (*Reader* 95). Unlike Lacan, who predicates symbolic discourse upon the separation from the mother, Kristeva argues that the dialectic between the semiotic—the preverbal discourse between mother and infant—and the symbolic constitutes poetic language (92–93). Thus the trace of the mother, as evidenced through the semiotic, plays an integral role in the construction of meaning and links symbolic language back to the physical body. This dialectic aptly describes the frequent collisions between bodies and words, silence and speech, in Faulkner's fiction. In fact, given that language is born out of the body, the two turn out to be not so separate, and even dialectics between them break down, erasing the distinction between the literal and figurative, allowing Addie Bundren to speak after her physical death.

Though primarily defined through their bodies, women can also exert figurative as well as literal power; the psychological presence of the mother extends beyond an emphasis on the physical body. Nancy Chodorow, in her now-famous study of mothering, asserts that "because of their mothering by women, girls come to experience themselves as less separate than boys, as having more permeable ego boundaries" (93). Since girls then grow up to be mothers, this sense of connection and fluidity becomes associated with the mother. Therefore, robbing the mother can also be seen as appropriating her permeability, her ability to break down rigid boundaries of the self. This fluidity comes across physically, in Addie's rotting corpse, and psychologically, in the ways that characters often seem to lose individual autonomy. Quentin, having robbed Miss Rosa of her tale by appropriating it for his own ends, comes to realize, "*Yes, we are both Father. Or maybe Father and I are both Shreve, maybe it took Father and me both to make Shreve or Shreve and me both to make Father or maybe Thomas Sutpen to make all of us*" (*AA* 326–27). Despite Quentin's inquiries into which of the men "made" the others, what he identifies here is the dissolving identity that women represent. In a sense, his feminine intuition provides him access to the story, a story that, appropriately feminized, is carried to term in nine sections.

Clearly, robbing the mother has many connotations. It means taking over her literal creative power and coming to terms with the dissolving boundaries between self and other, semiotic and symbolic. It means recognizing that language, rather than replacing the symbiotic union with the mother, may reunite mother and child. While women more often employ this maternal discourse, it is not restricted to women writers, for it depends not on biological difference but on a recognition of the ways in which gender is culturally constructed and on a realization of the mother's literal and figurative power. Examining and challenging culturally accepted notions of femininity and difference challenges the masculine order of being in our patriarchal society, a feat that can be accomplished by both men and women.

Yet Faulkner, who appropriates it, does so with an overtone of fear and criminality. He aspires not to write like a mother but to rob her. His transgressive stance may help to account for the violence and distrust so often associated with the feminine in his work. Thus Addie Bundren comes across as a powerful and terrifying mother rather than a loving one, and the sexual appetites of Temple Drake and Joanna Burden come dangerously close to denying them human identity. Even so, a major source of Faulkner's genius rests in that tense and often hostile relationship with female sexuality and creativity. If he were less suspicious of the nature of language and gender, he would be a lesser writer. My feminist reading seeks neither to castigate nor to feminize him. Rather, it seeks to identify the ways that motherhood—in all its guises—informs and shapes his work.

This focus on maternal power opens up new perspectives in Faulkner criticism as well as expanding our options as critical readers. As Jacobus points out, feminist analysis extends outside the text at hand:

> The alterity of feminist reading is posited, not simply in opposition to masculinist reading, not simply as a move that carries off familiar readings and puts them to strange uses, but rather as a move that installs strangeness (femininity) within reading itself. Femininity can be defined as the uncanny difference of masculinity within and from itself: feminist reading (correspondingly) can be defined as the uncanny internal difference or division— the ambiguity—by which reading refuses phallogocentric identity as the measure of available meanings. (286)

Refusing "phallogocentric identity as the measure of available meanings" is necessary to get beyond reading *Absalom, Absalom!* as the story of Quentin Compson or Thomas Sutpen, the story of patriarchal genealogy. Central as this story may be, it neither encompasses the full range of *Absalom*'s complexity nor illustrates the full measure of Faulkner's achievement. To refuse phallogocentrism also means to get beyond the seemingly rational explanations provided by Mr. Compson, and to examine the perspective of mothers as well as fathers by listening more closely to the voices of Rosa, Clytie, and Judith.

By linking femininity to the uncanny, Jacobus points out some of the connections between feminine power and maternal power. Freud defines the uncanny as "that class of the terrifying which leads back to something long known to us, once very familiar" (123–24). As Sprengnether has illustrated, "the body of the (m)other is the very site of the uncanny," for it "represents both home and not home, presence and absence, the promise of plenitude and the certainty of loss" (232). The "once very familiar" mother's body threatens the very selfhood which it created. As the site of home and not-home, self and not-self, the mother represents the force against which individuals must define themselves. And, in a world like Faulkner's where self-definition is so problematic, the mother embodies a significant threat to being and to the language which both establishes and undermines that being.

As has become clear, the mother speaks many languages and takes on many different meanings. A precise definition of maternity and, particularly, of the role of the preoedipal mother in constructing identity and language proves difficult to pin down. Of the many views, three are particularly useful here. Nancy Chodorow's object-relations theory of how mothers reproduce themselves in their daughters identifies permeable ego boundaries as a feature of women and mothers. Far from celebrating such a trait as innately female, however, Chodorow seeks to eradicate it by advocating changes in the ways that women mother. For Faulkner, fluid identity is generally associated with femininity regardless of whether it occurs in men or women. Gender boundaries and gendered discourse collapse, as his examination of identity and language takes him beyond conventional categories and expectations.

Kristeva's dialectic between the semiotic and symbolic recognizes the role of the preoedipal mother by citing the semiotic as an integral component of poetic language. Yet she fails to challenge Lacan's assertion that symbolic language is associated with the father, and further, that culture is in fact predicated upon the symbolic. Thus she reifies women's exclusion from language and culture, except for the moments when the semiotic bubbles up to disrupt the symbolic. I find most useful the paradigm suggested by Jacobus and, in greater detail, Sprengnether, that locates the construction of the self not through the oedipus complex and its corresponding move into the realm of the father but through birth as the originating loss, thereby establishing the preoedipal mother as a primary figure. De-emphasizing the role of the oedipus construct, Sprengnether erases the gap which separates the mother from language and focuses more attention on the literal body of the mother.

All of these theories help to illuminate the pervasive role and power of the mother in Faulkner's work. While Kristeva's dialectic, which closely follows Lacan's phallogocentric paradigm, may have its limitations, it is a useful tool in analyzing the ways that Faulkner's male characters constantly seek to control women through language. That they invariably fail reveals, I would argue, Faulkner's own awareness that the mother can rule in both the semiotic and the symbolic, that the imprint of her body can be traced through a focus on the corporeal and the ways that it can impede individual autonomy. Her uncanny presence and absence destabilizes the world of his fiction, allowing him to examine the roots of its being. Robbing the mother brings in considerable spoils.

Yet insisting on the importance of maternity as a creative paradigm in the work of a male writer does invite some disturbing questions. In her essay "Mallarmé as Mother," Barbara Johnson examines how a male writer can take on a maternal role, questioning what that means for women in danger of being displaced altogether from the maternal function.

> Hence, a man whose work consists of questioning certain assumptions and structures of phallogocentrism—the determinability of meaning, the separability of binary opposites, the search for self-identity—would somehow appear to fill the maternal role better, more effectively, than a woman. To the extent that a critique of the paternal position involves a privileging of ambiguity, undecidability, and deferral—the deferral of both separation and merger—that critique is operating from the arena of the pre-oedipal mother. But the fact that the maternal function is wielded by men—indeed, that literature is one of the ways in which men have elaborated the maternal position—means that the silence of actual women is all the more effectively enforced. (141–42)

Clearly, Faulkner questions "certain assumptions and structures of phallogocentrism," aligning him with the realm of the preoedipal mother. Yet
in identifying Faulkner with the maternal, do we displace the women who
bear babies and somehow idealize the position of the mother, particularly
when filled by a man? Certainly in our culture men who "mother" receive
far more praise than women who do the same thing. Furthermore, as
many feminist scholars have noted, focusing on maternal "discourse" as
prediscursive, presymbolic, can reify the very gender roles which have
controlled our culture for so long.

But in his presentation of gender, language, and creativity, Faulkner
challenges conventional maternal stereotypes as much as he does patriarchal ones. In both illustrating the power of the mother and in breaking
down gender itself as a stable construct, he reveals the precariousness of
patriarchy's hold on cultural identity. Rather than reaffirming the traditional role of the mother, he demonstrates that maternity is only idealized
in socially powerless characters such as Dilsey. In fact, mothers threaten
life as much as they create it, engulf identity as much as they nourish it,
and endanger language as much as they originate it. Out of these tense
oppositions is born much of the artistic power of Faulkner's greatest
novels, a power which analyzes the ways in which gendered creativity is
perceived, constructed, and deconstructed.

Faulkner not only challenges patriarchal culture through the disruptive
presence of femininity, he also examines ways that race undermines male
dominance. In many ways, his attraction to and fear of maternal power
mirrors his problematic treatment of race. It is no accident that the
smooth, distended, indeed pregnant, balloon which threatens Thomas
Sutpen actually refers to an African American. The same culture which
relegates women's creativity to secondary status, while elevating men's,
also denies African Americans access to art by denying their claims to
intelligence and even personhood. Just as women's bodies often determine
their fates and identities by confronting them with their biological functions, so the bodies of African Americans become the site of their oppres-
sion in a racist world. My discussion of gender and maternity necessarily
takes into account the ways that race and racism contribute to the conditions which foster artistic creativity.

As a destabilizing force, race both parallels and intersects with gender to
challenge white patriarchal domination. Joe Christmas, of questionable
racial identity, thus becomes feminized by his perceived exclusion from the

white order. To be black is to be other in many of the same ways that to be female is to be other. Consequently, rather than confront a doubled other, Faulkner saves his most extensive examinations of racial identity for men such as Joe Christmas or Lucas Beauchamp, or for its impact on Thomas Sutpen's attempt to establish a white male dynasty. Apparently, women's sexuality and maternity pose significant enough threats to displace concerns of race, for while Toni Morrison's Sula announces, "I'm a woman and colored. Ain't that the same as being a man?" (*Sula* 142), Faulkner's African American women are not masculine so much as dehumanized, a "different species," as Clytie is designated by Rosa. With the exception of Clytie, black women receive scant attention as anything other than stereotyped mammies or sex objects; the separation of sexuality and maternity applies even more strongly to black women than to white women. Dilsey, one of Faulkner's favorite characters, loses not humanity but subjectivity, displaying an unbelievable selflessness in the service of those who abuse her. By relegating black women to the peripheries of his novels, Faulkner reveals his deep uneasiness with the combination of racial and sexual otherness, a possibility too threatening and too foreign for him to contemplate. Maternal power, tied to white cultural order, is exercised almost exclusively by white women.

Ultimately my project here is less theoretical than applied; while I hope to uncover new ways to speak of femininity and maternity, I am primarily interested in examining the ways in which Faulkner's texts reflect, challenge, and undermine established cultural paradigms. I do not argue author intentionality; rather, I argue that as a product of white bourgeois society Faulkner himself is necessarily inscribed by our dominant ideology of gender and family. An artist, however, whether consciously or unconsciously, questions the beliefs which underlie his or her culture and analyzes both the power and the limitations of such paradigms. The pervasiveness of phallogocentrism in Faulkner's work testifies to its centrality and durability. Despite my emphasis here on mothering, I by no means suggest that Faulkner does not have equally problematic and interesting relations with paternity and the Law of the Father. That subject, however, has been more thoroughly explored in Faulkner scholarship, particularly in the work of John Irwin and André Bleikasten. In figuring the mother as central to Faulkner's texts we discover a source that is different but equally important.[1]

Though I begin with Faulkner's earlier novels, this book does not follow the chronological order of his work. Instead, I trace the growing impact of women's physical bodies and their figurative and linguistic power. Chapter 2 examines *The Sound and the Fury* and *As I Lay Dying,* investigating the mother as absent center. Both books, predicated on women's bodily absence, illustrate men's attempts to reconstruct the sister/mother linguistically, and to bury—either figuratively or literally—the mother's body. In Chapter 3 I deal with the excessive bodily presence and "aberrant" sexuality of Temple Drake in *Sanctuary* and Eula Varner in *The Hamlet,* looking at the ways these women's bodies are regarded as threats to the social order. Chapter 4, on *Light and August* and *The Wild Palms,* examines feminine duality in the pairs of women presented, and the attempted division of sexuality and maternity, literal and figurative. Finally, in Chapter 5, I explore the role of women in *Absalom, Absalom!* and the ways that the presentation of maternal power transcends the division of sexuality and maternity. The absent mother is deflected and displaced into a kind of "notmother," whose creative power extends far beyond the reaches of any other novel.

Faulkner's women, so often derided and castigated by both critics and other characters, embody the tensions out of which fiction is made. "The women that have been unpleasant characters in my books were not created to be unpleasant characters, let alone unpleasant women. They were used as implements, instruments, to tell a story" (*Lion* 125). More than instruments, many of his women provide the artistic source for stories in which, as Faulkner says, "I was trying to talk about people" (*Univ.* 10).

Chapter 2

Erasing and Inventing Motherhood

The Sound and the Fury and *As I Lay Dying*

In 1946 Random House reprinted *The Sound and the Fury* and *As I Lay Dying* in one Modern Library volume, a decision which caused Faulkner some distress: "It's as though we were saying 'This is a versatile guy; he can write in the same stream of consciousness style about princes and then about peasants'" (*Letters* 228). Despite his concern at being typed as a writer with a single prose style, this pairing makes sense, for the two books have much in common beyond their narrative structures. Faulkner may have labored long, hard, and lovingly over *Sound and the Fury* and written *As I Lay Dying* as a tour de force in only six weeks, but both books reverberate with the paradoxical power of women's bodily absence and presence, of women's silence and language. Both examine men's desperate attempts to deal with maternal absence, to use language as a replacement for the mother. Caddy and Addie, caught in a world which vanquishes women's bodies, nonetheless exert a powerful control over the literal and figurative, bodies and language, forcing brothers and sons to confront the fragility of their egos in the face of maternal power.

Faulkner's inspiration for *The Sound and the Fury* is well known. Most of his remarks about the genesis of his favorite novel center on Caddy, his "heart's darling," the "beautiful and tragic little girl" who was created to compensate for the sister he never had and the infant daughter he was to lose (*Univ.* 6; "Intro." 710). Other comments also locate Caddy at the center of the novel, as he claimed that the central image of the book was the picture of three brothers looking up the tree at their sister's muddy drawers (*Lion* 245). Yet Caddy, who forms the core of the novel, is never actualized in the text, which "grows out of and refers back to an empty center," as André Bleikasten puts it (*Failure* 51). That center—Caddy herself—in its simultaneous absence and presence marks Faulkner's first major attempt to confront the relation between gender and art, between female sexuality and narrative authority, between mothers and language. If Caddy is the empty center, then Faulkner has robbed the novel of its mother by robbing the mother of her voice.

This is not a novel about Caddy, despite Faulkner's claims, but about her brothers' responses to her, about how men deal with women and sexuality. In fact, Faulkner's almost obssessive insistence on Caddy's importance begins to sound defensive, an apology, perhaps, for essentially writing her out of the text. Caddy's linguistic absence from the novel undercuts her centrality in a text formed and sustained by voice. If she is his heart's darling, why does she not rate a section of the novel, the chance to tell her own story? But Faulkner goes further than just silencing Caddy; he ties her silence to her beauty, her femininity, and claims that "Caddy was still to me too beautiful and too moving to reduce her to telling what was going on, that it would be more passionate to see her through somebody else's eyes" (*Univ.* 1). David Minter has suggested that Faulkner found "indirection" a useful strategy "for approaching forbidden scenes, uttering forbidden words, committtting dangerous acts" (103). Yet the "forbidden words" and "dangerous acts" appear not to be Caddy's but those of her brothers: Quentin's incestuous desires, Jason's criminality, and Benjy's groping for the language "to say" which culminates in attempted rape. Indirection may approach male forbidden desires, but it does not approach Caddy except as the object of those desires.

Particularly in Faulkner's work, however, silence does not necessarily confer marginality. Paul Lilly has called Caddy's silence "a hallmark of the perfect language that Faulkner the artist knows can never be realized but which he knows he must keep on 'working, trying again' to reach" (174). But why must it be women who speak the perfect silence instead of language, even imperfect language? Linda Wagner argues that, despite their full or partial silences, Caddy and her mother control the narrative:

> Linguistic theory would define the narrator of any fiction as the person whose speech act dominates the telling of the fiction, yet Caddy and Car-

oline Compson are in many ways essential narrators of the Compson story. So much of their language, so much of their verbal presence, emanates through the novel that they are clearly and vividly drawn. Rather than being given one section, they take the novel entire. (61)

They are indeed "clearly and vividly drawn." Yet the fact remains that they are drawn rather than draw-ers, constructed rather than constructor, while the Compson brothers draw not only themselves but also "their" women.

Caddy's voice may never be restored, but the evidence of her physical substance remains. If her "speech act" does not dominate the text, her creative act does. Caddy's presence makes itself known less through her voice than through her body and its literal replication. Her physical pro-creation essentially engenders the linguistic acts which form the novel, thereby making this text, in a sense, her child. Yet it is difficult to claim that she "mothers" the novel when the process of mothering—and, particularly, Caddy's participation in that process—is hardly presented within the book as a triumphant creative experience. Her abandonment of her daughter to Jason and his malicious exploitation seriously undermines both her idealized status and her maternal position. While she serves as an admirable if temporary mother to Benjy, her treatment of Miss Quentin merits her no consideration as Mother of the Year. Faulkner has robbed the mother not just of her voice but her maternity. Because the brothers control the terms of the narrative, Caddy exists as sister rather than mother.

The problem, however, is that she serves as a mother as well, not just to Benjy but to all of her brothers, who find themselves confronted with problematic maternal ties to both their biological and symbolic mothers. Thus while their narratives, except for Jason's, lack the overt condemnation of Caddy which they all display towards Caroline (and even Jason saves his strongest complaints for Miss Quentin, displacing much of his resentment toward Caddy onto her daughter), they also reveal their unbreakable ties to Caddy, ties which deny them full control over their own identities. By his indirection, Faulkner has allowed Caddy to approach the position of all-powerful and all-encroaching mother rather than simply mother of Miss Quentin. Doubly abandoned, first by Caroline and then by Caddy, the Compson men achieve a kind of revenge in fixing both, in allowing each woman to be defined only through the perspective of her son/brother.

They fail to score a significant victory, however, because just as each brother inscribes his vision of Caddy, he also finds himself defined through his own relation to her. Quentin is trapped by being the weaker older brother to a powerful sister, by his own attraction to her, and by his sexual innocence as opposed to her experience:

> youve never done that have you
> what done what
> that what I have what I did (174)

Jason struggles against his sense of being unimportant and unloved, the brother whom Caddy never valued. Benjy cannot perceive himself as anything other than connected to Caddy, as his entire life constitutes an elegy of her loss. As both a presence and absence, Caddy's maternity determines the fate of the Compson family.

The novel, in fact, is full of mothers; besides Caroline and Caddy, we also have Dilsey, Frony, and Damuddy. But Damuddy dies before we ever meet her, and Frony, Luster's mother, functions as a daughter rather than a mother. Dilsey, more a mammy than a mother, primarily mothers ungracious and unappreciative children she did not give birth to: the Compson children and Luster. Thus, there are at once too many and too few mothers in this novel. These replacements, substitutions, and reversals in the function of mothering all undermine Faulkner's professed admiration for Caddy by linking her most disturbingly to her own mother—and to the failure of mothering, which holds such a crucial position in this text.

The lack of adequate mothering, as so many scholars have noted, causes many of the problems within the Compson family. Quentin's often quoted remark, "*if I'd just had a mother so I could say Mother Mother*" (197), lays the blame for his numerous problems squarely at Caroline Compson's feet, a reading many critics tend to uphold. Interestingly, Mr. Compson's alcoholic disregard for his family finds much more sympathetic treatment. Lack of adequate fathering is apparently not seen in as nefarious a light.[1] Even Thomas Sutpen, surely one of the worst fathers in literary history, is granted a Faustian grandeur which Caroline Compson certainly lacks. While Faulkner may overtly distance his "heart's darling" from such a problematic function, enough symbolic connections remain to call her idealized position into question. If even Caddy fails as an adequate mother, can there be any hope left in motherhood, or is the dungeon mother herself, as Quentin says? (198). The fact that we see remarkably little of

Caddy once she becomes a mother—only a few glimpses from Jason, the most hostile of the narrators—suggests that Faulkner was chiefly concerned with Caddy prior to maternity, before she becomes wholly identified as female; as a child, not only does she lack sexual maturity but she genders herself as male: "she never was a queen or a fairy she was always a king or a giant or a general" (198). In growing up she loses her childhood appeal and her sexual innocence as she moves toward femininity and motherhood.

Indeed, what chiefly disturbs her family about Caddy's motherhood appears to be the sexual activity that generates it, for Western culture idealizes mothers but condemns female sexuality. As Julia Kristeva has pointed out in "Stabat Mater" (*Reader*), the cornerstone of Christianity is the virgin mother, an icon perpetuated by a patriarchal system in an effort to deny women's sexuality as a necessary ingredient of motherhood. Faulkner, with his interest in unravished brides, seems well aware of the difficulties inherent in attempting to privilege both virginity and motherhood. Quentin quotes his father as remarking that "it was men invented virginity not women" (89). This closely resembles Addie Bundren's comment in *As I Lay Dying,* that men invented motherhood (157). These inventions serve to define women by their sexual status and yet avoid female sexuality itself as women's identifying characteristic, for virginity and motherhood exist in relation to male possession, male sexuality. Before a woman can become a mother, a position of considerable power, she must bear the cultural mark of male domination: a wedding ring. These labels control a woman's body until she herself comes under the control of a man. One can see why men, and not women, invented them.

Quentin finds, however, that the invention doesn't work. Imposing such terms as virginity and motherhood may construct a cultural discourse regarding the role of female sexuality, but it does not restrict women's bodies to their linguistic functions, as Mr. Compson realizes. "Women are never virgins. Purity is a negative state and therefore contrary to nature. It's nature is hurting you not Caddy and I said That's just words and he said So is virginity" (132–33). Virginity, a lack, a "negative state," is "just words," thereby implying that language itself represents a lack and explaining why all the language of the Compsons can never replace Caddy's loss. In identifying women, nature, and sexuality as distinct from "just words," Mr. Compson inscribes a cultural split between women and language and yet retains the words which have proved ineffectual, the words, which

Addie Bundren says, "dont ever fit even what they are trying to say at" (*AILD* 157). This, then, explains why female sexuality and, by extension, motherhood, are so threatening. They represent something that cannot be controlled, or even defined, by symbolic discourse. Madelon Sprengnether asserts, "At the heart of phallogocentrism lies the terror as well as the certainty of its own undoing. And this undoing is associated with the body of a woman, who must be controlled, who must be prevented from achieving a condition of power from which she can exercise this threat" (244).

The Compson men fail, of course, to control the woman's body. Consequently, in the face of Caddy's sexuality, they are left to confront their own impotence and undoing. Warwick Wadlington has observed that Caddy "represents the deathly alienation of experience for each brother, the passions that should be theirs rather than inflicted on them" (98). She has robbed them of their masculinity and hence of their cultural identities. The Compson brothers take refuge in discourse, using language in an attempt to recover what is irreparably lost—the narcissistic union with the mother, in this case figured as the sister. As Shoshana Felman notes, an incestuous desire for the sister can represent a "fantasy of a return to the womb, to femininity as mother" (40). Cut off from both mother and sister, forced to experience himself as separate, each brother in his narrative finds that language only leads to further alienation and ultimately, to a nonbeing similar to an embryonic state.

Benjy, who appears never to have left that embryonic state, comes as close as anything can to expressing what is essentially unrepresentable—what Kristeva terms semiotic discourse, the prediscursive communication with the mother. As far as we know, Benjy verbalizes only whimpers and bellows. Indeed, though constrained by the need to use symbolic discourse to present Benjy's interior thoughts, Faulkner strips as much reasoning power as possible from his language. When Benjy describes golf, he presents exactly what he sees. "Through the fence, between the curling flower spaces, I could see them hitting" (3). Likewise, when Luster closes the stove door Benjy notes, "The long wire came across my shoulder, and the fire went away" (67). Benjy's focus on the literal vision, his inability to deduce meaning, links him to the semiotic *chora*, Kristeva's term borrowed from Plato, to describe the mode which "precedes and underlies figuration" (*Reader* 94). His mental deficiencies render him unable to conceive of language as a symbolic structure; for him, it is a literal expression of what he sees and hears.

Because he cannot use symbolic discourse to replace his lost sister/mother, he formulates Caddy not through language but, as John Matthews suggests, through objects like the slipper, the cushion, and the fire (72). While his association of Caddy with these things does suggest the presence of some sort of imaginative process, it does not succeed in its attempt to replace the thing—Caddy—with a symbol, because the symbol lacks reality for him. It only evokes Caddy; it does not restore her. Faulkner claimed in the Appendix that Benjy remembers not his sister but only her loss. Rather, to remember Caddy is both to possess and to lose her. Thus he is trapped between union and separation. Because he cannot substitute language for his prediscursive tie to Caddy, he cannot enter into the Law of the Father, where reality is discursive.

Indeed, he is horribly punished for his one attempt to speak, when he supposedly attacks the girl at the fence. "I was trying to say, and I caught her, trying to say, and she screamed and I was trying to say" (60). Benjy's attempt "to say" is interpreted as—and may very well be—attempted rape. Jason immediately has him castrated, a fact of which Benjy is well aware. "*I got undressed and I looked at myself, and I began to cry. Hush, Luster said. Looking for them aint going to do no good. They're gone*" (84). Benjy here recognizes and mourns his fate; he realizes he can never enter into manhood and an autonomous identity, and his only response—crying—further grounds him in semiotic discourse. Language, which should subsume this phase according to Lacan, leading Benjy to the realm of the Father, instead relegates him to the prediscursive sphere of the mother and keeps him there, mute and castrated.

Yet Benjy comes closer than either Quentin or Jason to recovering Caddy in his semiotic discourse, precisely because he does not rely on an attempted verbal reconstitution. He does not use the language of the Father to return to the sister/mother, but rather evokes her through objects. By refusing to accept symbolic discourse in lieu of Caddy he may perpetuate her loss, but he also maintains a constant sense of her physical presence because he never displaces her. In addition, he perceives time not as linear but as a mode of repetition and eternity, which Kristeva identifies as women's time (*Reader* 191). Caddy is both always lost and always present. Thus it is only through techniques associated with femininity that Benjy can re-evoke Caddy. But lest we be too ready to construe this as a triumph on his part, it is important to remember that his "success" leaves him emmeshed in an eternal stasis. The inability to get beyond the semiotic leads to psychosis. Benjy needs not to dissolve into Caddy but to achieve a psychological separation from her, a move he never accomplishes. Without access to voice, he cannot construct an autonomous self and remains, despite Caddy's claim to the contrary, a "poor baby" (9).

Quentin, unlike Benjy, does attempt to take refuge in symbolic discourse, but the maternal semiotic constantly threatens to engulf him. Though his father claims that virginity is just a word, Quentin cannot be comforted by language, for he expects both too much and too little of it. While Quentin can use language with considerable facility, it does not grant him masculine power, for he cannot assert himself as a man and a brother. He fails sexually in that he finds himself unable to make love to Caddy and unable to use the knife as a substitute: in a sexually charged scene he holds the knife to Caddy's throat but can't push it in. Neither can his language accomplish what his penis and phallus cannot, for after shakily ordering Dalton Ames to get out of town by sundown, he faints "like a girl" (186). Betrayed by his lack of masculinity, he also tries femininity, imagining himself as Dalton Ames's mother: "If I could have been his mother lying with open body lifted laughing, holding his father with my hand refraining, seeing, watching him die before he lived" (91). It is significant that only mothers have this power of life and death in Quentin's world. Not only does he want to be a mother, he imagines himself as woman resisting the temptation to which Caddy succumbs: holding off the man, denying procreation and thus motherhood. However, only as an imaginative fantasy can this possibility exist. The body of the mother is too powerful for Quentin.

Despite all his lengthy conversations with his father, some real, some apparently imagined, Quentin faces a constant threat of re-engulfment in the mother. His almost frenzied focus on words marks the degree of desperation in his struggle to control experience through language rather than bodies. He wants to erase Caddy's literal motherhood, so he can restore her to a male-constructed linguistic state: virginity. When he tries to force Caddy to articulate specifically her reasons for marrying, she replies, "*Do you want me to say it do you think that if I say it it wont be*" (140). Caddy recognizes that pregnancy is beyond language, something that need not be said. She also knows her brother well enough to realize that he wants to be able to contain experience in language, because language is just words—like virginity—and thus not physically real. Quentin's hope— that if Caddy can say it, "it wont be"—can be viewed as an attempt to widen the gap between the semiotic and the symbolic, to define reality symbolically rather than physically. Her language will replace the condition of her body. In order to protect himself from becoming engulfed by the feminine, he tries to shore up the foundations of symbolic discourse, knowing all the while that his attempt will be in vain.

His desperate need to confess to his father that he has committed incest, which probably occurs only in his imagination, can be read in similar terms:

> and he did you try to make her do it and i i was afraid to i was afraid she might and then it wouldnt have done any good but if i could tell you we did it would have been so and then the others wouldnt be so and then the world would roar away. (203)

While this passage reflects Quentin's fear that his impotence has caused Caddy's problems—"if I could tell you we did it would have been so and then the others wouldnt be so"—it also illustrates his further attempts to block out literal reality with language. If he could *say* we did it, then his problems would disappear, not necessarily because he did it, but because it would then become a linguistic rather than a sexual act, and language, Quentin hopes, triumphs over the body.

Unfortunately for him, he can neither say it nor do it. Unable to leave the semiotic behind and to establish himself firmly within the symbolic, he makes literal his non-being through suicide, a choice which aligns him even more closely to the mother, both in its literalization and in the method he selects. He chooses to drown, to return to the symbolic womb and thus transform it into a literal tomb. As Marsha Warren points out, he "attempts to (re)create himself by rejecting the Law of the Father (time) as the regulating agency of discourse, and entering the Body of the Mother (space), thereby recovering the maternal semiotic flux" (101). In the final pages of his narrative his language comes more and more to resemble Benjy's semiotic discourse, as grammar and punctuation vanish, revealing the fragile line between semiotic and symbolic. Symbolic discourse fails him, stripping him of the emblem of separation from the mother. Since he cannot "say Mother" and escape into language, he cannot differentiate himself from her.

Jason, however, can say a great deal. He appears to heed the warnings of his brothers' struggles to master language and opens his narrative with an aggressive verbal stance. "Once a bitch always a bitch, what I say. I says you're lucky if her playing out of school is all that worries you. I says she

ought to be down there in that kitchen right now" (206). Every time Jason
speaks, he reaffirms that act with an "I says." Often, he even breaks up a
paragraph of his own voice to inject an additional "I says." Unlike Benjy,
Jason does indeed say, or rather, says. He didn't go to Harvard, so he
learns neither "how to go for a swim at night without knowing how to
swim" (224–25) nor grammar, thereby undercutting some of the authority
of his speech. Indeed, his constant reiteration of both his speech act and
his own control over it—"*I* says"—bear considerable similarity to Quentin's attempts to find refuge in language, the extent of the effort revealing
the anxiety behind it.

One of the more obvious ways Jason seeks to control the power of the
mother is by assuming an overtly protective relation to his own mother. He
constantly reminds himself of the need to protect her, almost reveling in
her helplessness. Jason's concerns lie with "my Mother's name" rather than
the name of the Father (269). In claiming to defend his mother's position,
he is, of course, primarily defending his own, revealing his selfishness and
his lack of separation from his mother. Her battles are his because his
identity is hers. Despite his mother's contention that he is not a real
Compson, a remark that probably does little to soothe his concern over his
family status, Jason displays great concern over the behavior of his niece
due to his pride in the family he constantly disparages, a family defined by
blood. "I haven't got much pride, I cant afford it with a kitchen full of
niggers to feed and robbing the state asylum of its star freshman. Blood, I
says, governers and generals" (265). Just as Jason defines himself through
the family blood, so does he define Miss Quentin: "Like I say blood always
tells. If you've got blood like that in you, you'll do anything" (275). The
power of blood continues to haunt him when he encounters the old man
from the circus and falls down (similar to Quentin's fainting in front of
Dalton Ames), terrified that he might be bleeding.

> "Am I bleeding much?" he said. "The back of my head. Am I bleeding?" He
> was still saying that while he felt himself being propelled rapidly away
> . . ."Look at my head," he said. (359)

This excessive concern over blood, both as an actuality and as a metaphor,
suggests a concern with the body, particularly with the female body and its
bloody functions of menstruation and childbirth. Quentin displays a similar obsession in his attempts to clean the bloodstains off his tie before

committing suicide. In identifying blood as a source of trouble, both implicitly recognize the threat of women's bodies.

But Jason's response goes beyond his brothers' efforts to construct a linguistic refuge from the mother. Jason employs a combination of language and robbery. He robs his own mother of the thousand dollars she gives him to invest in Earl's store, and he robs Caddy of the child support she sends each month. Not content with simply robbing the mother, Jason also steals from his niece and surrogate daughter, Miss Quentin. For Jason, who has a more literal mind than Faulkner, robbing women means appropriating not their creativity but their cash. His first attempt to rob Caddy is linguistic, when he gives her a momentary glance of her daughter in exchange for one hundred dollars. Observing his own word to the letter—"I said see her a minute, didn't I?"—he is outraged when Caddy manages to circumvent his strategies: "I didn't have any more sense than to believe what they said" (236). In relying on literal meaning, he fails to consider that Caddy may have greater imaginative powers. Ever the tattletale, Jason resorts to telling mother. Only a mother has the power of interdiction needed to defeat a mother, and with Caroline's words behind him, he defies both Dilsey and Caddy: "I know you wont pay me any mind, but I reckon you'll do what Mother says" (238). Ironically, robbing the mother teaches him the value of the mother's voice. After this questionable victory, he moves from verbal tricks to simple robbery, tacitly admitting linguistic defeat.

Forced to recognize the vulnerability of his verbal aggression, Jason learns to rely more heavily on money than language. Just as losing the job at the bank costs him his manhood, in that it makes him a victim of his sister's sexuality, accumulating money—especially by robbing his niece—gives him a sense of potency and power. His one sexual relationship is conducted largely on a cash basis, and he has "every respect for a good honest whore" (269). Consequently, when Jason reads Lorraine's letter, he rather naively assumes she's telling the truth when she says she misses him because, as he notes, "Last time I gave her forty dollars" (222). Having established his potency and worth through his money, he cannot doubt her regard. Significantly, after Miss Quentin's theft, he again thinks of Lorraine, this time in very different terms: "He imagined himself in bed with her, only he was just lying beside her, pleading with her to help him, then he thought of the money again, and that he had been outwitted by a

woman, a girl. If he could just believe it was the man who had robbed him"
(355). Having already been defeated in the battle of language, he now loses
the battle of money—both to a woman. Thus he also loses his belief in his
sexual virility and is driven home, unable even to operate the car for which
he robbed his mother.

Jason, like his brothers, is rendered impotent in the face of feminine
power and, like them, discovers that language provides no refuge. Thus it
makes sense that Jason should be the one to calm Benjy in the final
paragraph, when he rushes over to send the buggy the right way around
the square. Jason, forced to confront his final defeat at the hands of
women, may recognize a stronger bond with his brothers than he has ever
felt before. "[C]ornice and façade flowed smoothly once more from left to
right; post and tree, window and doorway and signboard each in its
ordered place" (371). The flowing from left to right, possibly an emblem of
the reading process but of a literal rather than written text, imposes the
only order possible in world where men can neither master symbolic
discourse nor escape the semiotic. Language cannot control the maternal
presence because if one accepts the feminist premise that the maternal,
with its inherent division, gives rise, requoting Jacobus, to both the subject
and language, then the mother is not ruled by language but actually
controls it. As Minrose Gwin points out, Caddy is a "text which speaks
multiplicity, maternity, sexuality, and as such she retains not just one voice
but many" (46). The many voices of woman overwhelm the Compson
brothers who find in their own lack of differentiation from the feminine
the true threat of Caddy's transgression—we have looked on the female
outlaw and she is us. The body of the mother/sister, the "very site of the
uncanny," according to Sprengnether, denies masculine authority the power to order the world. The uncanny, a reminder of castration fears, quite
literally fulfills its threat in this novel, as all three brothers are rendered
impotent, unable to vanquish the spectral presence of a sister who represents home and not-home, self and not-self.

But what about the primary mother in the novel, Caroline Compson,
the character everyone loves to hate?[2] How much responsibility does she
bear for the disruptions within her family? A cold, selfish, complaining
woman, she neglects all of her children, including her later favorite, Jason,
who cries every night when he can no longer sleep with his grandmother.
Her maternal absence is largely filled by Caddy, but Caddy has no mater-

nal model, for her own mother has only indicated how to be a lady. She orders Caddy not to carry Benjy because it will ruin her back. "All of our women have prided themselves on their carriage. Do you want to look like a washerwoman" (72). Caddy should not spoil—love—Benjy; "Damuddy spoiled Jason that way and it took him two years to outgrow it" (73). No wonder Jason cries himself to sleep when his grandmother dies. Finally, when her daughter emerges into womanhood, Caroline wears black and goes into mourning after she sees Caddy kissing a boy. For a woman to express sexual desire is for her to be denied status as lady, and thus, as living entity: "I was taught that there is no halfway ground that a woman is either a lady or not" (118). By accepting no halfway ground, Caroline Compson denies the grounding of motherhood itself, which is predicated upon an essential duality. Having challenged and defied maternity, it comes as no surprise to discover that she refuses to let her motherhood get in the way of her ladyhood. "I'm a lady. You might not believe that from my offspring, but I am" (346).

After Caddy's transgression it is Caroline who judges her. It is Caroline who refuses to allow her to return home, and Caroline who will not permit her name to be spoken, thus reversing the strategy of her husband and son, who invent labels—virginity—in an attempt to control female sexuality. Mrs. Compson erases Caddy by refusing to name or label her; Caddy exists only through what she is not: a lady. If she is not a lady, she cannot be named. Names have great significance for Caroline Compson who insisted that Maury's name be changed to Benjamin when his mental disabilities became known. She strenuously objects to both "Caddy" and "Benjy" as names because "nicknames are vulgar. Only common people use them" (73). Jason, she repeatedly states, is the only one of her children who is a "real Bascomb"; the others are all Compson, that being the mark of their difference from her.

Caroline, the strongest proponent of the lady, who marries Caddy off in an attempt to prevent scandal, nonetheless resists the traditional expectations of how a married woman should behave: that she will take on her husband's name and define herself through him. Just as Rosa Coldfield will refuse to become an incubator for Sutpen sons, Caroline rejects the Compson identity. She may have married a Compson, but she has not become a Compson, insisting to the end that she is a lady and a Bascomb. While far from being a protofeminist, Mrs. Compson nevertheless undermines the patriarchal structure of marriage and motherhood somewhat differently, but no less significantly, than Caddy, who turns out to inherit more from her mother than the ability to procreate.

Addie Bundren displays what may seem a similar interest in names, particularly those of her husband and sons. "And when I would think *Cash* and *Darl* that way until their names would die and solidify into a shape and then fade away, I would say, All right. It doesn't matter. It doesn't matter what they call them" (*AILD* 159). Addie, a more complex character and mother, recognizes that names and labels cannot define, that "words are no good." But Caroline Compson, having thoroughly internalized the cult of southern gentility, clings to such labels—emblems of masculine discourse— as a means of separating herself from her family. She puts great faith in the power of language; by changing her son's name she denies his association with her brother and thus erases any equation of the Bascombs with idiocy. And by refusing to allow her daughter's name to be spoken she denies Caddy's identity as both mother and daughter.

In this focus on the power of the name, the label, Caroline achieves the kind of power for which her sons seek in vain. Despite her repeated claims that she'll soon be dead, she outlives both husband and eldest son. While Quentin cannot live in a world where virginity is just a word and Benjy is castrated for "trying to say," Caroline successfully "masters" a language which imposes limits and boundaries, interestingly enough, the language of the Father. Critics have long castigated Mrs. Compson for being un-motherly, but maybe she simply plays the wrong parental role. She takes over the position of the father, redefining the Compson family as the Bascombs. She is left with Jason, a "real" Bascomb, Benjy, whom she renamed, and young Quentin, nameless. If it is generally the father, as Bleikasten asserts, "who names, places, marks," Caroline Compson is a father par excellence (*Light* 87). While Mr. Compson wallows in alcoholic verbiage, unable to impose order or even to oppose his wife's interdiction against speaking Caddy's name, Mrs. Compson is redefining her family and her world. If Quentin wants someone to say "Mother Mother" to, maybe he should turn to his father.[3] In this novel, mothers are, above all else, survivors, certainly a feature that would attract the artist/robber. One robs the mother because she will always be there, controlling both procreation and language.

There is, of course, one other significant mother in this novel. Dilsey, identified by Sally Page as Faulkner's "ideal woman" (70), by David Williams and more recently Philip M. Weinstein as a madonna, has long been hailed as the novel's savior, the only truly admirable character in the book (Williams 11; Weinstein 7). Her warmth and endurance have endeared her to generations of readers, and, apparently, to Faulkner himself. But Faulkner and his readers tend to overlook the problematic issue of race in deifying the stereotype of the black mammy. The suggestion that African American women make the best mothers—especially to white children— reflects not an idealization of the mother or the black woman but a cultural disdain for both. Mothers are only "good" when socially powerless, when controlled by those they "mother," when selflessly dedicated to selfish undeserving children. A close examination of Dilsey's maternal halo reveals the inadequacy of white cultural assessments of mothering when applied to African American women.

Whence comes this halo? Certainly Dilsey appears to feel more compassion for the Compson children than any of their biological parents. She cares for Benjy, defies Jason in giving Caddy a chance to see her daughter, and protects Miss Quentin from physical abuse. Yet she cannot function as a mother to these children, not because she didn't give birth to them but because she lacks selfhood and power in a white racist world. "You damn old nigger," says Miss Quentin after Dilsey saves her from a beating (213). In calling attention to her race, and thus to her cultural powerlessness, Miss Quentin denies Dilsey maternal control. While Dilsey stands up to Jason, who seems to live in some fear of her, she makes no attempt to defy Mrs. Compson's selfish and inconsiderate demands, dedicating her life to the people who oppress her. In fact, she favors her white employers above her own family, granting Luster no hearing or compassion in his monumental task of caring for Benjy. Her selflessness confers sainthood upon her in the eyes of her white creator and a large portion of predominantly white readers. As Myra Jehlen points out, Dilsey's virtues "recall the traditional Mammy virtues Faulkner extolled in his own Mammy" (76). However, the novel Faulkner dedicated to his mammy, Caroline Barr, is not *Sound and the Fury* but *Go Down, Moses,* where Mollie Beachamp at least exerts herself for her own children and grandchildren, and where Lucas challenges white expectations of black mammies in his confrontation with Zach Edmonds. Faulkner pays Caroline Barr the compliment not only of the dedication but of the presentation of a black woman who comes across as less idealized and, ironically, less of a mammy than Dilsey.

On the other hand, Dilsey's idealized status as a madonna/mammy denies her both subjectivity and sexuality, and thus robs her of the mother's pervasive power, her control over being and language. The descriptions of her body focus on its decay, not its feminine appeal or procreative potential. She has a "collapsed face that gave the impression of the bones themselves being outside the flesh" (307). Dilsey's "indomitable skeleton" evokes only the body's framework, the mother's potential worn away by the oppressive demands of a racist culture.

The narrative strategy of the fourth section of the novel, sometimes called Dilsey's section, reconfirms her questionable status. If this is Dilsey's section, why does she not get a voice? If Caddy was too beautiful and too moving, is Dilsey too much of a madonna and not enough of a mother to speak? Thadious Davis suggests that the use of the third-person narrator here establishes "the perspective of time. Faulkner creates a sense of the passing of an era, and within that perspective he presents the destruction of one family and the endurance of another." Dilsey, Davis says, "exists as a kind of sacred vessel, suggesting an experience that is both visionary and tragic" (106). She may be a "visionary and tragic" vessel, but she is not a maternal vessel. Her lack of direct voice highlights her symbolic rather than her bodily role. Not until *Light in August* does Faulkner make his first serious attempt to deal with black subjectivity. And mothers, above all else, are subjects in Faulkner's work. Dilsey, possibly more a wish-fulfillment than a real character, more symbolic than human, may endure, but as an idealized image, not as a source of being and not-being, of language and separation—not, in other words, as a mother.

Faulkner said that his feeling on beginning to write *The Sound and the Fury* was, "Now I can make myself a vase like that which the old Roman kept at his bedside and wore the rim slowly away with kissing it" ("Intro." 710). Minter points out that this urn takes on multiple meanings: a haven, a feminine ideal, a work of art, and a burial urn. "If it is a mouth he may freely kiss, it is also a world in which he may find shelter; if it is a womb he may enter, it is also an urn in which his troubled spirit now finds temporary shelter and hopes to find lasting expression" (102). Re-entering the womb, however, may not be as benign as Minter suggests, particularly when we consider the experiences of the Compson brothers. But urn or womb, shelter or art, this vase clearly represents the novel Faulkner loved so much, a vessel which, the rim having worn down, disgorges its contents and overflows its boundaries. In short, it behaves like a woman and a mother.

In speaking of the feminine, Luce Irigaray cautions that while it is often defined as "lack, deficiency, or as imitation and negative image of the subject," it can also be characterized as "*disruptive excess*" capable of "jamming the theoretical machinery" (78). Certainly the maternal feminine presence fits this description. Caddy's disruptive excess jams the machinery of language and masculinity, neither able to hold off the feminine. Shoshana Felman observes that the feminine "is not *outside* the masculine, its reassuring canny *opposite,* it is *inside* the masculine, its *uncanny difference from itself*" (41). The Compson men find that the feminine within themselves leads to their own destruction. Wounded both physically and psychically, they lose life, language, and masculinity. Caddy may be doomed and her mother damned, but Quentin is killed off, Jason robbed (and thus figuratively castrated), and Benjy literally castrated in a text where the mother controls both literal being and figurative identity. Maternal power thus forges a novel of separation and loss out of the story of "a woman that cant name the father of her own child" (303). In this book, the name of the father gives way to the body of the mother.

> When he was born I knew that motherhood was invented
> by someone who had to have a word for it because the
> ones that had the children didn't care whether there was
> a word for it or not.
>
> (*AILD* 157)

Motherhood—invented by men, who use words, and accomplished by women, who use bodies—lies at the core of *As I Lay Dying,* highlighting the tension between literal and linguistic creativity. Both *The Sound and the Fury* and *As I Lay Dying* deal with absent mothers, but the absences have differing causes and implications. While *Sound* grows out of Caddy's maternity, *As I Lay Dying* is born out of Addie's death. A maternal corpse replaces maternal absence. Faulkner sets up two creative paradigms in the novel: mothering and speaking. What he does not do, however, is to set them in opposition to each other, with women as literal and men as figurative creators. After all, Addie's voice is strong enough to be heard through her coffin, and her son Darl achieves, at times, a kind of nonlinguistic "feminine" intuition.

The two dominant motifs in the book—corpse and voice—twist slightly the kind of dichotomy between the semiotic and symbolic presented in

Sound, for by placing the mother's literal dead body rather than the mother's absence in the center of the text, Faulkner grants greater power to the physical, while at the same time erasing its boundaries as the decaying corpse disperses its odor and its influence throughout the novel. Then, after finally getting the mother into the ground, returning her to the earth, the Bundrens are still left with Dewey Dell, defeated in her attempts to end her pregnancy, and presented with a second Mrs. Bundren. The mother's body, ultimately, cannot be vanquished. Neither does that body, a speaking corpse, give up control over language, thus reducing even further the division between physical and linguistic power. In fact, language in the novel is strongly tied to maternity. Just as the Compson brothers find symbolic discourse an inadequate replacement for the mother, so the Bundrens struggle in vain to fill her place with words and symbols. The mother's body and the mother's voice are vividly present, as Faulkner constructs a tale where even killing the mother does not silence her.[4]

Warwick Wadlington, examining the role of voice in Faulknerian tragedy, argues that voice "says No to death primordially: voice is the breath of life transformed through sound into communication, communion" (105). Certainly voice serves as one of—if not the—most important empowering forces in Faulkner's work. In this novel in particular, even the dead speak. Yet not only is that voice often disembodied, it is also often unspoken in a text which highlights the close connections between voice and silence. The "dark voicelessness" Addie experiences "in which the words are the deeds" (160) transforms language into action, taking it out of the realm of the spoken voice and into a prediscursive semiotic sphere. Thus the blurred boundaries between voice and silence resemble the collapsing distinction between between paternal and maternal discourse, between body and language. Does voice also say no to maternity, the primordial reality which precedes language, or does it emanate from the mother's body?

This novel, even more than *The Sound and the Fury,* focuses on voice; created out of its many speakers, *As I Lay Dying* attests to the power of spoken language but also insists, through its title, on the centrality of the body. The mother may die, but her body remains. Voice, however, proves a bit more evanescent, for the book frequently documents the characters' reluctance to employ verbal discourse. Darl and Dewey Dell communicate without words; Addie realizes that "words are no good" (157); Vardaman finds he "couldn't say it" when he understands that his mother is about to be placed in a coffin (59); Whitfield "frames" rather than speaks his confession. In order for voice to say no to death, one must use it as a vehicle for linguistic expression, a feat often left unaccomplished in this book.

But those who do place faith in language often find themselves deluded by their misguided beliefs in language's controlling power. Anse repeatedly announces, "I give her my promised word" (111), to justify a journey which costs Jewel a horse, Cash a leg, and Darl his freedom. Cora worries about losing the cost of the eggs that went into the cakes, for it was on her "say-so" that they bought the hens (5). Her daughter Kate resents the lady who changes her mind about buying them, insisting, "She ought to taken those cakes when she same as gave you her word" (6). This comic undercutting of the power of the word reveals Faulkner's skepticism regarding language's ability to represent "truth" and delineate human experience, reflecting his modernist agenda and tying him to another great modernist practitioner, Robert Frost. Whitfield's attempt to "frame" the words of his confession conjures up the final lines of Frost's "Oven Bird": "The question that he frames in all but words / Is what to make of a diminished thing."

To frame is not to speak, but to circumscribe, limit, and define a shape; in this novel, however, words, as Addie says, are "just a shape to fill a lack" (158). While filling and framing would seem to be antithetical operations, they do have a common element—both present language as a physical form, a characteristic, Irigaray claims, of women's language. "This 'style,' or 'writing,' of women . . . does not privilege sight; instead, it takes each figure back to its source, which is among other things *tactile*" (79). By conceiving words as "tactile," Faulkner ties language to the literal, to the body. Because words are cast *as* physical they cannot function as a replacement or substitution *for* the physical. Thus Faulkner's recognition of the limitations of language reflects the pervasive power of the mother both to enable and to inhibit symbolic discourse, to transform words into shapes and so to deny their purely symbolic nature.

When presented as abstract concepts, words, to Addie, only get in the way because they dangle like spiders, "swinging and twisting and never touching" (158), a mode which prevents true knowledge and intimacy. This can only be achieved through blood—when she whips her students or when she gives birth to Cash. Initially, she is exhilarated by the blood-letting of motherhood, believing that she has found an escape from symbolic discourse. Next to the experience of maternity, "words dont ever fit even what they are trying to say at" (157). Her blissful union with Cash exists beyond language: "Cash did not need to say it [love] to me nor I to him" (158). But her second pregnancy destroys her belief that motherhood's prediscursive communion heals the gap which words, "never touching," inscribe. Having once been "made whole again by the violation" (158) of childbirth, an additional childbirth re-violates her. She now recognizes that motherhood is as great a trick as language. "I realized that I had been tricked by words older than Anse or love" (158–59)—the word *motherhood,* invented by men but referring to an experience which predates language, the presence of prediscursive reality.

Betrayed by both the figurative word and the literal experience, Addie finds no comfort in maternity once it becomes repetitive. Where the inital act liberates her, the repetition entraps her. She seems to recognize the problem inherent in the feminist privileging of the maternal metaphor. As Domna Stanton explains, while this paradigm does value the female experience, it also reinforces the essential Law of the Father. The privileging of wombs over words still restricts women to their roles as wombs. Once, for Addie, motherhood provides a haven from symbolic discourse; twice, however, forces her to realize, Constance Pierce says, "the power of what has been as persistent an enemy as language: her own biology and her inevitable place in the biological scheme of things" (297). Despite her powerful control over the process of figurative thought, her body now defines her identity. She takes a final stand against maternal definition by returning to her own father, both symbolically in her realization that he "had been right," and literally in her insistence on being buried next to him (159).

But if Addie thinks she has abjured mothering by realigning herself with her father and his belief that "the reason for living is getting ready to stay dead," she is wrong (162). Her tie to her mother is even more compelling. Doreen Fowler points out, "If Addie's father 'planted' her, then Addie's mother is the land, in which the seed grows. But the mother herself is never named. She is the repressed referent, the origin that imbues all symbols with meaning, but is herself absent" ("Matricide" 116). This description could refer to the state which the Bundrens hope to impose on Addie: returned to the land, repressed, and, most of all, absent. But while Addie's mother may be the repressed unspoken referent, Addie herself is far more difficult to deny, at once mother and earth, present and absent. Not only does she live on as corpse rather than staying dead, but her maternal influence lives on in her children, further denying the finality of death. Thus though T. H. Adamowski has called Addie a "woman with a penis" (225), her womb exerts a far more powerful force over her life and the lives of those around her.

Rather than becoming a phallic mother, Addie rebels against both the language of the father and that of the mother. Not only do words take on physical shapes, they take on the feminine of the vessel: "I could see the word as a shape, a vessel." Gendering words as feminine, Addie uses them to transform abstract concepts into physical reality, then collapses the reality back into the abstract concept. "I would watch him [Anse] liquify and flow into it like cold molasses flowing out of the darkness into the vessel, until the jar stood full and motionless: a significant shape profoundly without life" (159). Words neither protect nor contain life; they, like the physical body, are subject to disintegration, as she repeats the names of her husband and sons "until their names would die and solidify into a shape and then fade away" (159). Words, as either figurative names or literal shapes, cannot cohere to their referents. As Addie phrases it, "I would think how words go straight up in a thin line, quick and harmless, and how terribly doing goes along the earth, clinging to it, so that after a while the two lines are too far apart for the same person to straddle from one to the other" (160). Though she sets up an opposition between the figurative and literal, her analysis is not quite accurate, for these two forms of discourse do intersect within her own body. Both die, and both share the same shape: the word, "a significant shape profoundly without life like an empty door frame" and the "shape of my body where I used to be a virgin" are empty vessels. Neither words nor virgin bodies produce life.

That the mother's body literally subsumes life and language, collapses literal and figurative, is absolutely appropriate for a novel in which the mother is both figured and embodied as a corpse. Emblemizing the dissolution of both bodies and language, Addie's corpse stands beyond the control of either literal or symbolic discourse, presenting a formidable challenge to the family that must repudiate it. Thus while the Compson brothers attempt to fill the gap Caddy leaves behind with language, in *As I Lay Dying,* where words, "profoundly without life," are too much a part of the mother's body to replace it, the Bundrens try to lessen the impact of Addie's death more through deeds and symbols. They must combine doing and language to deal with a body which has transcended both. Their struggles reflect the broader concerns of the novel which, says André Bleikasten, "interrogates the relationship—or lack of relationship—between world

and language" (*Ink* 202). This problematic connection intensifies the di-
lemma of Addie's children, who attempt to use a language that is "no
good" in achieving their separation from a mother's body which is all too
vividly present. The corpse, both origin and end, refuses to die. As Julia
Kristeva explains in *Powers of Horror*, "the corpse, the most sickening of
wastes, is a border that has encroached upon everything" (3).

Addie's corpse, which encroaches upon the family, the community, and
the novel, seems to encroach even upon the laws of physical dissolution
by refusing to go away. In fact, its prolonged existence is largely enabled
by the Bundrens' reluctance to consign it to the earth too quickly, despite
Samson's remark that "a woman that's been dead in a box four days, the
best way to respect her is to get her into the ground as quick as you
can" (102). Addie's extended existence as corpse denies the divisions between life and death and impedes the literal and symbolic transformation of mother to earth. The family's resistance to completing the process,
to consigning the body to the land, is illustrated by Vardaman's boring
holes in the coffin and Cash's care in removing the mud splashed on it, as
he "scours at the stain with the wet leaves" (96). While Vardaman attempts
to erase the coffin's boundaries and Cash to keep them proper, both act in
a way that reflects a denial of the mother's death; Vardaman wants to make
sure she can breathe, and Cash seems to feel that she would be disturbed
by a dirty coffin. Unable to articulate their feelings, to transform their
doing into language, they cannot yet understand that the mother now has a
figurative rather than a literal presence. Thus it is not just through Addie
that Faulkner illustrates the connections between bodies and language,
between maternal and patriarchal discourse. Her sons need to construct a
discourse of separation which is both literal and symbolic. They rely on
symbols which are physical objects rather than words. For Cash, the coffin that he so carefully constructs becomes the emblem of the mother,
while Jewel's horse functions as a clear mother substitute. Even young
Vardaman, struggling with metaphor in his famous line, "My mother is a
fish" (74), chooses a figure which is literal and which he himself has
killed.

As Fowler suggests, each of these symbolic substitutions "reenacts the
original separation from the mother, the cutting of the umbilical cord"
("Matricide" 117). But none of the separations seem to work, possibly
because these substitutions, rather than moving into language, remain
grounded in the realm of the physical. In fact, the objects are themselves

replaced, while the body of the mother remains present. Thus Jewel must sacrifice his horse, and the work Cash puts into the coffin is largely undone by Vardaman's drilling and by the wetting it receives in the river. Even Vardaman's fish disappears into "not-fish" (49), which is "cooked and et" (52). They must lose these symbols of the mother and reconnect themselves literally to the mother's body before the final burial of the mother can be achieved. Cash, with his broken leg, lies on the coffin itself for several days, Jewel carries the coffin out of the burning barn singlehandedly, and Vardaman moves from denial—*"My mother is not in the box. My mother does not smell like that"* (182)—to acceptance that the coffin does contain the body of his mother for he "can hear her" (197) through the wood and "can smell her" (199). The failure of their symbolic substitutions forces them to realize that the process of figuration—even using literal objects—will not displace the mother. Only a literal burial can accomplish that, and that burial cannot occur until they have sacrificed their symbolic replacements and carried out the mother's final law: that she be buried in Jefferson.

The daughter, however, has a different experience. Not only does Dewey Dell have no time "to let her die" (106), she heals the separation at the moment of death, as "she flings herself across Addie Bundren's knees, clutching her, shaking her with the furious strength of the young before sprawling suddenly across the handful of rotten bones that Addie Bundren left" (44). Gabriele Schwab points out that Dewey Dell "literally buries that body under her own sensual corporeality. In this image mother and daughter melt into a dark version of a grotesque 'pregnant death'" (213). Having buried the mother well before the epic journey begins, Dewey Dell has no need to replace the mother figuratively, for she literally replicates the mother in her own pregnancy. In both burying and reproducing the mother with her own body, she eschews language, and rather than speaking "begins to keen," expressing herself not in symbolic discourse but through a prediscursive semiotic non-language (44).

In fact, Dewey Dell communicates without needing verbal discourse, saying of Darl's knowledge of her pregnancy: "He said he knew without the words . . . and I knew he knew because if he had said he knew with the words I would not have believed that he had been there and saw us" (24). The wording foreshadows Faulkner's later experiments with what, in *Absalom, Absalom!,* he would term "notlanguage." By the time of *Absalom,* Faulkner had become much more daring and sophisticated in his representation of nonlinguistic communication, for there the characters never do learn the actual truth in words; the best approximation to what might be the truth is an unverified intuitive leap by Quentin. But in *As I Lay Dying* this unspoken discourse is confirmed: we know from Dewey Dell that she is pregnant and from Darl that he knows it. Why, then, would Faulkner choose this "notlanguage" if he is not, as in *Absalom,* challenging the possibility of ever truly knowing?

The answer lies in the nature of the subject at hand. Pregnancy, like motherhood, cannot be "invented" with words, can be established only through experience, that is, through the body. If Faulkner is not yet ready to launch a full-scale attack on the power of symbolic discourse, he does recognize that there may be conditions, such as pregnancy, in which such discourse is rendered obsolete. Body language and symbolic discourse compete for dominance in a book which, Eric Sundquist writes, "is obsessively concerned with problems of disembodiment" (29), and in which "acts of speech" should be interpreted "as partially or wholly detached from the bodily selves that appear to utter them" (30). By separating speech from body, Faulkner allows for multiple permutations of the relations between them. It is women, however, who seem most aware of the choices inherent in such a division.

Dewey Dell, though she lacks her mother's more philosophic recognition of language's limitations, views it with suspicion and takes every opportunity to avoid using it. In a conversation which strongly recalls that between Caddy and Quentin, Darl says to her,

> The reason you will not say it is, when you say it, even to yourself, you will know it is true: is that it? But you know it is true now. I can almost tell you the day when you knew it is true. Why wont you say it, even to yourself? (35)

While Quentin hoped that if Caddy could "say it," it wouldn't be true, Dewey Dell seems to recognize that once she says it, she will know that it *is* true. Contrary to Quentin, who wants to replace the physical pregnancy with words, Dewey Dell recognizes that language has no such power to eradicate the body. Language merely verifies what she already knows "is true now." Her feeble hope to stave off knowledge of her condition lacks the almost insane force with which Quentin makes a similar demand. Dewey Dell, as Darl understands, is simply refusing to articulate what her body has already told her. Though by this silence she fails to ask Dr.

Peabody for an abortion and thereby loses what may be her only chance to avert maternity, she does go to considerable lengths—short of literally saying it—in her quest to end her pregnancy.

Dewey Dell's response, then, to both impending motherhood and the death of the mother, is to refuse to put her thoughts and feelings into words. She keens or she stays quiet, in each case resisting the movement into symbolic discourse, the movement away from the mother. Instead, she throws herself upon the mother and finds herself unable to pronounce the words which might get her an abortion, thus ensuring that she will replicate rather than replace the body of the mother. Trapped by the physical, she feels, "It's like everything in the world for me is inside a tub full of guts" (53). Women's lives, as she realizes, are literally shaped by their bodies.

"For the same reason that women are identified with nature and matter in any traditional thematics of gender," writes Margaret Homans, "women are also identified with the literal, the absent referent in our predominant myth of language. From the point of view of this myth, the literal both makes possible and endangers the figurative structures of literature" (4). Addie's procreation, her doing, has engendered the need for her sons to find words to gain autonomy from her, and her death, another doing, reconfronts them with what they are trying to separate from: quite literally, the earth. Likewise, we see in Dewey Dell the literal which both births and threatens the figurative. By re-embodying the mother she reinvents motherhood and yet also confirms the fear that one can never escape the mother's body; like Hydra's heads, it replicates itself unendingly in the face of death.

Despite Dewey Dell's strong identification with the natural world, she does, of course, speak as well. Yet her language, even when she appears to speak metaphorically, is language of the body, the literal: "He is a big tub of guts and I am a little tub of guts" (53); "I am my guts. And I am Lafe's guts" (54). Dewey Dell expresses her pregnancy both literally and metaphorically in these remarks. To say that she is now both her "guts" and "Lafe's guts" is, of course, quite accurate. Her words display significant facility with language, challenging her exclusion from the figurative. Yet Dewey Dell does have difficulty with simple expression; she never once articulates her condition directly and, in fact, displaces her own fertility onto the natural world: "I feel like a wet seed wild in the hot blind earth" (58). Thus while she clearly has been identified with the physical, with nature, her association with literal discourse seems problematic; she is unable to speak the literal truth and expresses herself, despite her language of the physical, figuratively. Dewey Dell, the creation of a male author, both displays and challenges modes of discourse associated with women. She uses language which is both figurative and tactile, trying to see Vardaman's face, to "feel it with my eyes" (57). Her transformation of vision into touch recalls the prediscursive relation between mother and child, linking her to the maternal even in her language.

Dewey Dell's facility with language, however, exists only as unspoken. More than her brothers, who frequently express themselves aloud as well as within their own minds, she has great difficulty speaking. Even Vardaman, struggling to find the words to deal with his mother's death, has several conversations about it with Darl. Dewey Dell's silence, as much as her tactile and physical diction, defines her feminine status. Only Darl can read her mind, though she vainly hopes that Dr. Peabody will cross the language barrier and answer her unspoken request. "He could do every-thing for me if he just knowed it" (53). Because she cannot "master" speech and persuade someone to give her an abortion, she is relegated to silence and thus to pregnancy and motherhood. Indeed, she finds herself in this predicament precisely due to her decision to allow a physical circum-stance—whether or not her cotton sack is full at the end of the row—to determine her sexual actions. She communicates with Lafe primarily sen-sually and physically: "our eyes would drown together touching on his hands and my hands and I didn't say anything" (23–24). Her silent acqui-escence to Lafe's determination to beat chance by picking into her sack seals her fate. Dewey Dell's nonverbal communication, a kind of semiotic discourse, restricts her to her maternal function. One needs oral expression to challenge, and possibly hold off, maternity. Even her desperation to find an abortion-inducing drug does not facilitate her speech. The druggist Moseley first sees her "just standing there with her head turned this way and her eyes full on me and kind of blank too, like she was waiting for a sign" (183). However, signs—the symbolic—will not erase her physical condition.

It is tempting to read Dewey Dell's pregnancy, like Lena Grove's, as an emblem of hope. Moseley rebukes her search for an abortion, telling her,

You get that notion out of your head. The Lord gave you what you have, even if He did use the devil to do it; you let Him take it away from you if it's

His will to do so. You go on back to Lafe and you and him take that ten dollars and get married with it. (188)

Amid all this pro-life and pro-Lafe rhetoric, one can forget that for Dewey Dell, this pregnancy is a violation. She has been violated by Lafe, by MacGowen, and by Darl, when he sees her and thus invades her privacy. Pregnancy, rather than confirming her abilities to procreate life, denies her control over her own life and her own body. Her pregnancy results from her acquiescence in removing herself from her identity, in allowing her own disembodiment. "I said if the sack is full when we get to the woods it wont be me" (23). She refuses to accept responsibility for her decision and to participate in her own sexuality: "it wont be me." By denying her body she denies her identity, for if she is not Dewey Dell, she becomes simply sexuality embodied, as, indeed, many scholars have labeled her.[5] Yet once again, there is more to her language than denial; she eerily foreshadows her own position as expectant mother by realizing that once her "sack" is full, it won't be her. Once pregnant, Dewey Dell loses human identity, and is described by Darl as a "leg coming long from beneath her tightening dress: that lever which moves the world; one of that caliper which measures the length and breadth of life" (91). He later comments that one can see, shaped by her wet dress, "those mammalian ludicrosities which are the horizons and the valleys of the earth" (150).

But to accept this reading, however persuasive, that she represents the life of the physical earth, the literal, is to ignore her recognition of how it denies her very being. She feels that if Dr. Peabody could give her an abortion, "then I would not be alone. Then I could be all right alone" (53). She would not be alone because Peabody would share her trouble. But, more importantly, she would not be alone because she would regain her self, her identity; then, she would be "all right alone," having healed the lack within herself. Far from granting life, pregnancy robs her of being: "I feel my body, my bones and flesh beginning to part and open upon the alone, and the process of coming unalone is terrible" (56). No wonder she displays such animosity towards Darl, whose thoughts she seems to be very well able to read, for his rhetoric inscribes pregnancy as life-embodying rather than self-denying.

Darl's reading of pregnancy as a force beyond the body, as an embodiment of life itself, is understandable given his own problematic relationship with his mother, which causes him to doubt the existence of literal mothers. He reads motherhood figuratively rather than literally, realizing that he never had a mother, but "Jewel's mother is a horse" (89). While Dewey Dell never fully separates from the mother due to her gender, Darl never breaks away because he was never mothered, was never really a part of her. Thus Darl takes on a kind of feminine identity, one which may contribute to his growing insanity. He is capable of nonverbal communication, which sets him apart from the other men in the novel. Darl sees and understands things that others do not. As Tull says, "It's like he had got into the inside of you, someway. Like somehow you was looking at yourself and your doings outen his eyes" (111). Not only does his body lack clear boundaries, but it is also associated with the "land [which] runs out of Darl's eyes" (106).

His ability to overflow his physical boundaries and his weakening grasp on his own identity, which deteriorates to the point of speaking of himself in the third person, in some ways mirror Dewey Dell's denial of herself when she removes herself from the sexual act. The fluid ego boundary, Nancy Chodorow has argued, is a feature of women, whose identities are not constructed on difference from the mother but on similarity. When applied to Darl, however, the effect is devastating. Dewey Dell's ability to step outside herself reinforces her sexual identity as it facilitates the act which results in her pregnancy. Dewey Dell is driven into her body, but Darl is out of his mind by this division of self. His intrusion into the minds of both Dewey Dell and Jewel proves so serious a threat that they conspire to commit him. Women often suffer drastic fates when forced to live in a male-oriented system. Darl demonstrates how a man's participation in a female experience may be equally dangerous. Time and again, Faulkner demonstrates the problems of categorizing gender roles, though focusing less often on the women than on the men driven mad by the need to be manly men.

Darl, who seems to float through a world of words, passing into people's minds and crossing vast spaces at will—such as when he narrates the scene of Addie's death from miles away—lacks the stability to fix an identity. The one who produced him failed to mother him; as he says, "I cannot love my mother because I have no mother" (84). Because Darl lacks a stable ego, he lacks stable ego boundaries, leaving him with the fluidity of the mother without her prediscursive power. He uses figurative discourse with great facility but never attempts to construct a figurative replacement for the mother, possibly because he never had a mother to replace. He simply wants to destroy her remains. Thus his poetic and metaphoric language lacks purpose and definition, undermining his position within the realm of the father; he has nothing against which to define himself.

Both Fowler and Bleikasten grant Darl honorary maternal status. Fowler claims "he is like the mother" ("Matricide" 122), while Bleikasten notes "in many ways he *is* his mother. His gaze is hers—not reembodied, but disembodied, excarnated" (*Ink* 188). Darl's disembodiment is critical, however, for it marks his lack of procreative power. He may be *like* the mother, but he is producing no babies, no life. To be identified with the mother is deadly in this book. Just as his gaze becomes "excarnated," so too does his identity, leaving him only with insane laughter, "our brother Darl in a cage in Jackson" (236). When Darl tries to substitute doing for words, when he burns down Gillespie's barn in order literally to destroy the body of the mother, he reveals his inability to function within the literal world; for Darl, to *do* is to threaten both symbolic law and cultural law. Committed to the asylum for his doing, he is expelled from family and from sanity. That Darl, the most articulate and perceptive character in the book, cannot survive illustrates the limitations of disembodied language, of functioning linguistically rather than physically.

Though Darl vanishes with a burst of insane laughter, Cash remains behind, realizing that "this world is not his world" (242), yet still wondering whether "ere a man has the right to say what is crazy and what aint" (221). Cash, the careful craftsman who seems to replace Darl as the artist/narrator by the end of the novel, shares some of Darl's mind-reading capabilities. As he and Darl watch Jewel ride his horse across the river, Darl thinks, "When he was born, he had a bad time of it. Ma would sit in the lamplight, holding him on a pillow on her lap." Cash immediately responds to this thought by saying, "That pillow was longer than him" (130). But while this interchange reveals some fluid ego boundaries, it primarily reflects the intimacy between the two brothers (as Cash says, "It's because me and him was born close together" (217)) more than it suggests an intrusion into another's thoughts; each simply understands what the other may be thinking. Unlike Darl, Cash remains grounded in his body, undergoing considerable physical pain to complete the journey. Though tempted, at the river, to feel relief at the possibility of getting rid of the corpse, he recognizes the function of the ritual, of putting the mother's body to rest physically and symbolically.

If completing the ceremony grants Cash autonomy and artistic power,

Jewel the satisfaction of honoring his mother's last request, Vardaman and Dewey Dell some bananas, and Anse a new wife, it would appear that the mother has finally been vanquished, that she ceases to control and order the family. But if the mother's body no longer grounds the family, neither does symbolic discourse, for with the loss of Addie and Darl, we lose the two characters most able to use language with grace and facility. What remains is Dewey Dell's pregnancy, suggesting that, despite the burial of the mother, maternity seems to triumph over language. Yet Faulkner is far from reducing the creative tension between the literal and linguistic to a simple victory for motherhood. Motherhood breeds isolation rather than communion, and, for Dewey Dell, it represents her failure to employ symbolic discourse as a means of averting maternity. She is a mother by default, not by choice. The juxtapositioning of the corpse of the mother with the mother-to-be further undercuts privileging of motherhood. On one hand, we can say that the cycle continues: the mother is dead, long live the mother. But the continuation reinforces women's subjection, both to words, such as love and motherhood, and to wombs.

Both figurative and literal conspire to entrap women in motherhood. Yet in revealing his awareness of the problematic nature of both modes of discourse, Faulkner aligns himself with women writers through his manipulation of this dichotomy. One of the several ways that Homans identifies through which women writers express ambivalence about myths of language which separate and privilege the figurative is the literalization of the figurative. If figurative discourse is essentially masculine, literalizing it makes it more feminine. "Such literalizations of figures," Homans writes, "especially when connected to female themes, articulate a woman writer's ambivalent turning toward female linguistic practices and yet at the same time associating such a choice with danger and death" (30). One reproduces the figurative but recognizes its cost to women. Addie's statement, "He is my cross and he will be my salvation. He will save me from the water and from the fire" (154), becomes literalized when Jewel rescues the coffin from the river and the burning barn. Yet the statement, as Cora realizes, is perilous; "out of the vanity of her heart she had spoken sacrilege." Addie's literalization rewrites the Word of God, and thus constitutes a serious challenge to patriarchal discourse.

The challenge, however, is limited, for the literalization of this figure depends on Addie being in her coffin. In literalizing the word of God the Father, making Jewel her savior, Addie also literalizes herself from soul to corpse. The decaying body is as literal and natural as one can get: the person gone beyond language to what we might call a post-discursive reality. But that corpse also becomes an emblem; each family member displaces onto the dead mother the true meaning for his or her journey. The ostensible motive—to bury the mother in town—gives way to many not-so-hidden agendas: Anse wants new teeth and a new wife, Cash a phonograph, Dewey Dell her abortion, Vardaman to see the train in the store window and to eat bananas. Even Jewel has a deeper motive in his need to bury his mother figuratively as well as literally. This transformation of corpse into symbol allows the family to construct a discourse for the journey and to put up with physical hardships ranging from floods to the sickening odor of the decaying body.

The two who fail to construct a symbolic substitute for the mother, Dewey Dell and Darl, pay the highest price. For Dewey Dell, this trip does not even bury the mother; rather, it ensures the survival of motherhood in her failure to abort her fetus. Darl, who not only fails to construct a discourse for the journey but who does his best to prevent it by taking Jewel and the team away just before Addie's death, by not trying to save the coffin from the river, and by burning down the barn, pays even more dearly, sacrificed to the family's need to re-establish its identity as grounded in culture rather than corpse. "It wasn't nothing else to do. It was either send him to Jackson, or have Gillespie sue us" (215). Significantly, this situation results from the one time Dewey Dell does use verbal expression and tells Gillespie of Darl's guilt, despite her warning to Vardaman to say nothing. In this move into symbolic discourse she sacrifices not just her brother but a part of herself: "I always kind of had a idea that him and Dewey Dell kind of knowed things betwixt them. If I'd a said it was ere a one of us she liked better than ere a other, I'd a said it was Darl" (220). But in expelling Darl, who knows of and in some ways shares her pregnancy, Dewey Dell succeeds in ridding herself only of the figurative emblem of her violation, not the fetus—and thus not the maternity.

Finally, despite all the linguistic anguish in the novel, all the words which "go straight up in a thin line, quick and harmless," it is maternity that cannot be vanquished. The mother's body—the crossing between literal and figurative, patriarchal and maternal discourse, controls the journey and the text. Ultimately, the power of this novel lies in the ways these two creative paradigms both challenge and reinforce each other. The reliance on words and wombs highlights their intersection, a possibility which only women can fulfill. Men may invent motherhood, but women, who embody it, also encroach upon the invented word.

Women's bodies, whether present or absent, exert considerable power in both of these novels, mocking male impotence and challenging male control of figurative expression. If excluded—until after death—from symbolic language, they at least ensure that language will provide no refuge from maternal engulfment. The absent maternal presence collapses the distinctions between presence and absence, literal and figurative, bodies and language, transgressing upon individual identity and, ultimately, being itself. Dead, violated, or exiled, these women embody the tensions out of which art is made, as the mother exacts the price for the "Ode on a Grecian Urn."

Chapter 3

Sexuality, Inhumanity, and Violation

Sanctuary and *The Hamlet*

*S*anctuary and *The Hamlet,* while differing widely in tone and form, both focus on women's bodies and sexual violation. Unlike *The Sound and the Fury* and *As I Lay Dying,* which are predicated upon women's bodily absence, in these two novels female bodies dominate the action. Maternal presence and power, however, take significantly different form in these texts. While sexuality in both novels looms more threateningly than maternity, women elicit similar dichotomies between literal and figurative discourse. The influence of the maternal is felt as much in its impact on language as in the physical presence of the mother. In each book, maternity and the female sexuality behind it pose serious threats to male autonomy and the cultural order.

Written shortly after *Sound,* with *As I Lay Dying* sandwiched between its two drafts, *Sanctuary* at first glance seems markedly different. It lacks the narrative innovation and the intense investigation of family relations. Yet in several significant ways it closely resembles the other two novels, for, as John Bassett points out, it focuses on family and the home, drawing "parallels between domestic and social corruption, violence and loss" (74). Furthermore, he argues that *Sanctuary,* like *Sound and the Fury* and *As I Lay Dying,* "explores the myth of virginity, the fear of sexuality, the dichotomy in which women are either madonna/virgins or sexual objects" (73). But Faulkner's approach here differs significantly; while he investigates female sexuality, there seems to be much less respect for women in this novel. Both Caddy and Addie wield tremendous influence; Temple's sole exercise of power appears to be her perjury at the end. Victimized and wished dead, she lacks their imaginative force and hence, the sympathy accorded them. Completing the female lineup, we have Narcissa Benbow Sartoris, far less interesting than she appears in *Flags in the Dust,* and Ruby Lamar, an idealized madonna/prostitute, virtually powerless even to mother her ailing child. Obviously, this is not a novel with strong women characters; it is, however, a novel with a strong feminine presence, a presence which challenges and undermines the Law of the Father, as language proves inadequate to rein in feminine power. The tensions and contradictions regarding women in this often uneven novel come through in the many collisions between and among bodies and language, literal and figurative, law and nature. Ultimately, Faulkner challenges the definitions not just of gender but of humanity.

Sanctuary, with its focus on the horrific and sensational, presents a confused and contradictory picture of women and of sexuality. Despite male impotence and female insatiability, women end up being the victims of sexual abuse because male sexuality is a tool, an often-disembodied power which can be transferred to corncobs or other men. Female sexuality, on the other hand, rests solely in the female body and, as Temple discovers when she tries to turn herself into a man, is nontransferable. Not only are women defined by their sexual bodies, but those bodies are characterized as animalistic and inhuman. Temple, in the throes of sexual desire, is compared to "a dying fish" (252), while Miss Reba reconstructs herself and Mr. Binford in her two dogs. Amid this degradation of human female sexuality, women such as Narcissa, who hope to prosper and gain respect, must deny their bodies and enter in to a material world based on law and language.

Such a denial can be difficult, for in *Sanctuary,* as André Bleikasten argues, "the focus is primarily on what happens to, in, and between bodies" (*Ink* 237). Given the association between mothering and the body, this physicality suggests that the "maternal subtext" can be unearthed by reading the language of the body. "What calls for our immediate attention here," says Bleikasten, "is not so much the characters' words, thoughts, or feelings as the silent language of their bodies, the mute text written into the novel through their postures, gestures, and motions." The "silent language" of the body evokes Kristeva's semiotic or Irigaray's prediscursive reality, both associated with the feminine. While reading bodies may uncover feminine expression, it is difficult to argue that the focus on the body redeems the largely negative portrayal of women, because women's bodies are so violated in this novel. What is uncovered is not so much women's hidden strength as men's weakness and the fragility of patriarchal authority. The "mute text" of the body speaks the inadequacy of masculine law and culture, of discourse, and of conventional family structures.

Weak bodies and stunted development reflect the failure of the family to foster autonomous individuals. From Horace Benbow's adolescent revulsion to sexuality expressed through his wretching, to Temple Drake's body being "more compatible with eight or ten" than seventeen (73), to Popeye's physical impotence and fear of the dark, to Tommy's feeblemindedness, evidenced by his "rapt, empty gaze" and his cheek bulging "innocently by a peppermint jawbreaker" (117), the book hosts a cast of characters who appear never to have grown into adulthood. While one could blame both mothers and fathers for this prolonged childhood, the end result illustrates the instability of what should be the realm of maturity, that of the Law of the Father, the world of law, order, and language. Certainly the literal and surrogate fathers in the novel display little evidence of power or control. Horace is a painfully inadequate stepfather to Little Belle; Popeye, though called "Daddy," will never be able to claim that title legitimately, his impotence a legacy from his own syphilitic father; Judge Drake's name does not save Temple from the rape, nor does his influence protect her from the public humiliation of the trial. Clearly, the father fails in his culturally appointed role as establisher of familial and social order. Fatherhood loses both its symbolic and its literal power, becoming nothing but another fiction.

The most vivid portrayal of the father's weakness emerges in Pap's regression back into infancy. Both his name and his physical condition reflect his infantile status, which is further enforced by Ruby's care of him. The conflation of father and infant produces a blind, deaf old man with a stained beard, whose "cataracted eyes looked like two clots of phlegm" and who "regurgitate[s]" his tobacco into a rag (13). While the emphasis on his body and his inability to control basic physical actions associate him with the child's prediscursive relation to the mother, the references to his cataracts, white hair, and beard degrade the innocence of childhood into the shame of senility. He seems to combine a prediscursive and postdiscursive position, doubly excluded from a position of true patriarchal power. Yet Pap is not only the patriarch of the house, but as the oldest male present, with his long white beard, he becomes a pathetic parody of God the Father, which Faulkner underscores by having Temple call upon him at the moment of her rape. "'Something is happening to me!' she screamed at him, sitting in his chair in the sunlight" (107).

Temple's prayer is hardly compelling; here, the blind and ineffectual God offers no response. Earlier, when trying to pray, "she could not think of a single designation for the heavenly father, so she began to say 'My father's a judge; my father's a judge' over and over" (55). That Temple finds herself unable even to name god indicates both the degree to which she is excluded from the symbolic and the fragility of that realm. If the Name of the Father represents the symbolic order, ruled by language, then the fact that God the Father remains unnameable reveals a gap at the center of the symbolic, a gap within the very language which should compensate for that unattainable signifier, the mother. Given this symbolic failure, it comes as no surprise that the unholy trinity of fathers—"the heavenly father," the judge, Pap—fail her in this world of paternal and divine absence. None of them can save her from the man who will never be a father.

Daughters are left not only unprotected by the father but vulnerable to him, for fathers in this novel, as John N. Duvall notes, seem to have incestuous attractions to their daughters and function as the "excluded voyeuristic third in the sexual relation between his daughter and her lover" (63). Horace drools over Little Belle, Ruby's father kills her lover Frank, asking her, "Do you want it too?" (61), a question with an overt sexual overtone. Popeye, Temple's "Daddy," derives sexual pleasure from watching Temple and Red perform. But not only do they fail as fathers, they also fail as lovers, defeated by their bodies and left only with the name of father.

This name of father falls short of the Lacanian Law of the Father, for the father's defeat is closely tied to the failure of language, as the characters find themselves unable either to articulate their feelings or to use language to order experience. Popeye, never a man of many words, refuses to speak up to defend himself at the end; Lee will not speak to save his life; Temple seems largely unable to express openly her fears and desires and finds only "parrotlike" (300) language with which to condemn Goodwin (her one exception is the vivid description of her night of "comparative inviolation" [225], to be discussed later); and finally, all of Horace's language fails to accomplish his aims. His success as a lawyer largely depends on rhetorical skill, but he can barely speak, even to object, once Temple takes the witness stand. The most eloquent expression of his feelings is his wretching after hearing Temple's story and associating her with Little Belle. If entering in to the Law of the Father means mastering symbolic discourse, the characters of *Sanctuary* live as paternal outlaws. They speak, but their verbal language pales next to "the silent language of their bodies."

Faulkner's insistence on the absence and/or inefficacy of the father and his discourse would seem to leave the field open for mothers. While fatherhood tends to be distanced and ineffective, not just figurative but fictional, motherhood is present in the flesh. That flesh, however, may prove as weak as the spirit of the father in fulfilling its parental function. But are all of these failed and essentially mute adults testimony to failed fathers or failed mothers? Bleikasten, in a somewhat contradictory manner, both exonerates and accuses mothers for producing all of these unnatural children: "The key to Popeye's absurd and criminal fate is in his unerasable childhood, and childhood lies at the core of all evil in *Sanctuary*. Not 'Cherchez la femme!' but rather 'Cherchez l'enfant!' And look for the mute mother behind" (*Ink* 255–56). After seemingly excusing "la femme," Bleikasten's comment that the "mute mother" lies behind the evil of childhood suggests that the mother *is* in some way responsible, either because the mother is always to blame or because her muteness makes her an accessory to the crimes and language of the father.

But just how mute—or how powerful—is the mother? Faulkner presents us with a culture whose disdain for women colors its perception of maternity, for women, after all, are mothers. Of the two literal mothers in the novel only one, Ruby Goodwin, comes across as particularly maternal. While Ruby at times seems, like Dilsey, to wear a maternal halo, quietly tending to her sick child, there are also moments when her qualifications for the role of madonna come under comic fire. She keeps her son in a box "so the rats cant get to him" (19). The child is far from having been immaculately conceived, as she has prostituted herself more than once and appears willing to do so again should Horace request her services in payment of his legal aid. She is surprisingly harsh to Temple, out of sexual jealousy over Goodwin's interest and class resentment of Temple's privileged life. Yet despite all this, Ruby comes off as possibly the most admirable character in the novel, certainly as the most appealing woman.

The reasons for this are telling. First of all, she sticks by her man, sacrificing even her body for his sake. Accepting female sexuality as defining her power and position, she uses it for men's benefit rather than her own and now lives in poverty and monogamy rather than in luxury and promiscuity. Her attitude differentiates her from Temple, who seems to derive an inhuman pleasure from the sexual act and, moreover, seems to use her body for her own ends in an attempt to gain Red's assistance. Thus Ruby is no threat to the male hierarchy; not only does she recognize her role as one which sexually services men, she has also fulfilled the other patriarchally approved female function, which is to produce a son. No matter that the child appears unlikely to survive beyond its first year; Ruby has affirmed, through her body, patriarchal continuity. She is a "good" mother, selflessly dedicated to her son and his father. She appears not very successful at the job of mothering and qualifies as a good mother only insofar as she is selfless, not because she is particularly good at it. As a weak yet dedicated mother, she does not threaten individual identity.

Thus Ruby becomes a mother without the often terrifying power associated with the mother in other novels. Because of her class status, her promiscuity lacks the chaotic force of Caddy Compson's, and she seems to lack Addie Bundren's philosophical questioning of maternity and language. Unlike Lena Grove or Eula Varner, Ruby can scarcely be seen as an earth mother, with her ailing child and her nightgown of "faded pink crepe, lace-trimmed, laundered and laundered until . . . the lace was a fibrous mass" (80). She defines herself through the men in her life and seems to feel proud of the brutality she has suffered both by and for them. Ruby's very selflessness, her dedication to her men, distances her sexuality, making it less threatening. Generally in Faulkner's work, feminine sexuality is dangerous when it threatens family and/or male identity. But Goodwin, though he beats her for prostituting herself for his benefit, seems to have little invested in either Ruby's identity or her sexuality. His concern should he die is focused on his son; Ruby, he feels, will be better off without him. "She might have hung on with me until she was too old to hustle a good man. If you'll just promise to get the kid a newspaper grift when he's old enough to make change, I'll be easy in my mind" (286). She can continue to trade on her body, but the child merits consideration.

It is the women of the community who sense Ruby's destructive potential, as she realizes from the start. When she first meets Temple she immediately classifies her: "Honest women. Too good to have anything to do with common people. . . .But just let you get into a jam, then who do you come crying to? to us, the ones that are not good enough to lace the judge's almighty shoes" (60–61). When Horace decides that he can no longer offer shelter to Ruby, she understands immediately, possibly even better than he does: "You have kinfolks here, though. Women. That used to live in this house. . . .It's all right. I know how it is" (126). Ruby knows what her presence means to "good women" as the "church ladies" chase her even out of the hotel. "It's them ladies. You know how it is, once they get set on a thing. A man might just as well give up and do like they *say*" (189; my emphasis). Church ladies who campaign to suppress bodily expression can speak with authority because their privileging of the verbal over the physical fits the laws of this patriarchal culture.

The women are particularly threatened by Ruby because they see in her the fragility of their own positions. The only thing separating her from them is marriage. Giving her body without demanding legal marital status in return sets a dangerous precedent by undermining the institution which determines women's place. Thus she presents the possibility of women losing their primary legal, social, and personal identity and being relegated to bodies. Because these "honest women" have accepted law—and its vehicle, language—as an ordering principle, to deny the necessity of marriage is to deny them their place in the world. Once Ruby eschews legal status, she is reduced to her body and conforms not to the laws of men but to the laws of nature who, according to Horace, is a "she" (16). Ruby, operating outside of the law, explodes the notion that law controls society and thus threatens the women who live by manipulating it: Narcissa, who manages to circumvent her brother's case, and Miss Reba, who, when not drunkenly grieving over Mr. Binford, runs a prosperous brothel.

Interestingly, despite their shady legal dealings, these women are not only tolerated but valued, for both seek to impose restrictions on female sexuality, Narcissa through preaching morality and Miss Reba by commodifying women's bodies. Miss Reba numbers bankers, lawyers, doctors, and police captains among her customers, thereby establishing a kind of legal credibility. As she tells Temple, "Anybody in Memphis can tell you who Reba Rivers is. Ask any man on the street, cop or not" (149). Prostitution is sanctioned and protected because it controls female sexuality, reducing it to a product for male consumption. Thus law, based on a set of written rules, proves unable to establish consistent order; it can be put aside when it serves men's purposes to do so. In particular, laws protecting women's bodies lack force. Whorehouses prosper, patronized by lawyers and police captains. Later, the district attorney's assurance to Temple—

"Let these good men, these fathers and husbands, hear what you have to say and right your wrong for you" (299)—collapses in the face of comments by the men of the town: "I wouldn't have used no cob" (309) and "We got to protect our girls. Might need them ourselves" (313). There are no laws to protect women from this verbal aggression, from the assumption that they are commodities for men's pleasure.

Yet men and the law display a marked illiteracy when it comes to reading those bodies as anything other than sexual vessels. Thus Temple's verbal perjury prevails even though her body language, as she stares in terror toward the back of the courtroom "at once detached and cringing" (299), belies the brief replies which condemn Goodwin. Apparently, women's bodies are to be used and not read. Thus they fall outside of the law which comes into being linguistically, established, as Margaret Homans suggests in her reading of the *Oresteia,* to pardon matricide. Law may suppress maternal power, but Faulkner documents the failure of the law in a novel akin to Dickens's *Bleak House* in its indictment of the legal profession, suggesting that the mother may not be as dead as the lawgivers have assumed. Her remains, like Addie Bundren's, exert a powerful influence. Mothers' bodies prove very difficult to vanquish. Even legally sanctioned mothers like Narcissa, who try to leave their bodies behind, display an affinity for the physical and literal.

Narcissa, though the mother of a ten-year-old son, appears untouched by her maternity. In her "customary white dress," entertaining her collegiate suitor Gowan Stevens, she gives the impression of being a young girl, a still-unravished notbride (26). While Ruby's distanced sexuality results from selflessness and dedication to men, Narcissa's seems more a product of selfishness. Yet because it is associated with virginity, she becomes a prize to be won rather than an aberration or threat. Like Ruby, she has produced a son and, like Ruby, she lacks the kind of strength and power Faulkner generally attributes to mothers. But Narcissa's ostensible lack of maternal power is linked to the ways in which she tends to privilege masculine forms of discourse. She, unlike Horace, knows how to win in court. Narcissa speaks less with her body than with her words and deeds. She is, in fact, a better man than her brother. Yet Narcissa moves between figurative and literal modes of thought, a more complex character than we might initially suppose. As so often happens with Faulkner's women, there is a great deal beneath the surface of her stupid serenity. She both participates in and rejects motherhood, speaks and acts, functions as object and subject.

In many ways it appears that Narcissa has been defined by her body. She has an air of "serene and stupid impregnability" (110) and lives "a life of serene vegetation like perpetual corn or wheat in a sheltered garden instead of a field" (111). The use of the word "impregnability" both affirms and questions Narcissa's status as "perpetual corn or wheat"; if she is impregnable, how can she be perpetual? On the other hand, if she is perpetual she need not be pregnable. The inherent contradiction is, in fact, entirely appropriate, for this seemingly virgin mother has perpetuated herself without losing her impregnability. Though identified with nature, she lives in a "sheltered garden." The implication is of weakness, dependence, a plant which can only survive when sheltered and protected. That shelter and protection are provided, of course, by the chivalric tradition, by gentlemen who have a stake in separating pregnability and perpetuation and who control women's nature by sheltering it. In this characteristic Faulknerian division between sexuality and motherhood, we see an attempt to keep Narcissa young and impregnable, to focus not on her body but on her white dress, symbol of the purity she no longer possesses.

In her preference for younger men, Narcissa appears to support this cultural image of herself. Her widowhood wipes out her sexual past, and, no longer owned by any man, she is free to regress into a prelapsarian state, to return to the garden. Yet it is precisely her maternity which prevents this. Her brother's cynical comment, "She seems to like children" (24), proves false when she rejects Gowan's proposal because "one child was enough for her" (173). She has mothered a son; she declines to mother a husband. She appears to realize in advance what Addie Bundren learns in her second pregnancy: that repeating motherhood traps women in a biological function. Narcissa, who seems to prefer the cultural order to the natural order, perpetuates herself as a virgin, that state, as Mr. Compson would say, which is contrary to the state of nature.

Yet if Narcissa refuses this maternal role, she retains a tremendous respect for the memory of her own parents and her own birth, or more particularly, for the location associated with them. She shows surprising vehemence in her reaction to Horace's bringing Ruby into their childhood home. "The house where my father and mother and your father and mother, the house where I—I wont have it. I wont have it" (122). Diane Roberts has recently suggested that due to "Narcissa's linking of her self with the parental home," Ruby's intrusion into the house constitutes one of the rapes in the novel (27–28). Narcissa's deflection of her own identity

onto the family home highlights the tremendous importance of place in a
novel filled with violated sanctuaries. From the Old Frenchman place to
the Memphis brothel, space, as Bleikasten observes,

> offers no shelter. It is not meant to be inhabited; no one can feel at home in
> it. Like time, it is experienced as *expropriation*—alien, treacherous, whirl-
> ing, and dizzying, a space with ever shifting boundaries . . . a space which
> appears either as a threatening outside or as a suffocating inside. (*Ink* 227)

If place "is not meant to be inhabited," it may be said to move from the
realm of the physical to that of the symbolic. For Narcissa that house is not
so much space as it is symbol, a figurative rather than a literal spot.

Or rather, she would prefer it to remain figurative, and for this to occur,
it needs to remain empty. Shortly after Horace moves in, she drives up and
presumably enters, since the two of them hold a conversation (although it
is perfectly plausible that the conversation be held out by the car). But that
entrance—if it occurs at all—is fleeting, and Narcissa never returns to the
house, sending Isom instead with supplies and messages. Thus she herself
resists violating this space. She objects to Horace's moving in even before
he offers shelter to Ruby, clearly preferring the house to remain vacant. It
serves her as a sanctuary only when it is off-limits, an empty vessel. This
need to have the house physically conform to her figurative desire reveals
the degree to which she remains caught in the literal. She cannot literally
re-create (and re-populate) her ancestral home and seems to be able to find
solace in the thought of it only as a signifier rather than a signified, an idea
rather than a house. Narcissa cannot erase the literal picture of Ruby in the
house, cannot function wholly in the symbolic realm. This space "is not
meant to be inhabited" because habitation moves it from the figurative to
the literal.

In fact, as Roberts suggests, that space becomes more than just physical,
it becomes Narcissa's own body. Her revulsion at the idea of anyone—
even Horace—intruding into it clearly indicates the degree to which she
identifies with this empty space. Narcissa, who appears not to want to
repeat motherhood, finds this empty vessel a desirable reflection of her
own empty womb. What we see here is a conflation of the literal and
figurative. While the physical condition of the house is crucial, the house
itself acts as a symbolic representation of Narcissa's body. It becomes alien
when actually used as space, once it becomes physical. Thus Narcissa's
sense of identity is strongly tied to the literal reflection of her body.

Yet we must not overlook her desire to sell the house "when Benbow married the divorced wife of a man named Mitchell and moved to Kinston" (110). Given that Faulkner specifies not just Horace's leaving town, but his marriage to a divorcee, it is evident that Narcissa's desire to sell is based not just on practicality but also on a sense of betrayal of the family. Once Horace defiles the sanctity of family, the family home seems to lose its appeal, and Narcissa simply wants to rid herself of the symbol of what no longer exists. While she may show more wisdom in wishing to sell than Horace, who cannot bring himself to break his ties to the symbolic home, as long as she remains a legal owner of the house, it continues to function symbolically for her. Both brother and sister believe in the ties between legal and sentimental attachment, between literal and figurative connections. Yet, due largely to their respective genders, the symbolic meaning of the house affects them differently. For Horace, returning to the house is, in some ways, a return to the womb. He comes back to escape an unsatisfactory marriage, to return to the life he used to lead. Given his gender, however, perceiving the house as womb is purely figurative. He does not see himself literally embodied in the structure. Narcissa, quite accurately, does.

This empty house evokes the urn imagery so often gendered as feminine in Faulkner's work, and thus functions as a female space. Houses, after all, generally belong to the woman's sphere. Even the Old Frenchman place, which "lifted its stark square bulk against the failing sky" (7), evoking a slight phallic association, is a place devoid of traditional masculine activity: "But nowhere was any sign of husbandry—plow or tool; in no direction was a planted field in sight" (43). In detailing the lack of "husbandry," Faulkner subtly suggests that the place is emasculated; certainly if Popeye, Tommy, and Pap are any indication, the symbolism works. Though the house may be named after the old French*man*, its fields have not been planted, another metaphor suggesting male impotence. Even the self-proclaimed owner, Lee Goodwin, exerts little authority, and is beaten to the rape by Popeye despite Tommy's promotional advertising: "Lee says hit wont hurt you none. All you got to do is lay down" (104).

The old Frenchman place's symbolic emasculation does not, however, necessarily make it feminine. In the original draft of the novel, Faulkner specified that the house lacked a woman's touch:

It never occurred to Horace that there would be a woman there; there was that about the bleak ruin which precluded femininity. It was like coming

upon one of those antediluvian thighbones or ribcages which flout credulity
by its very fragmentary majesty and from which they reconstruct an organization too grandly executed to have housed such trivial things as comfort
and happiness and nagging and affection. As though whatever women had
ever dwelled there had been no more than a part of the vanished pageantry
of a dream. (OS 51)

If women are associated with comfort and happiness, then Horace's assumption that there are no women present at the Old Frenchman place
should be accurate. But it isn't. While this place may not house "comfort
and happiness and nagging and affection," it does house a woman.

Interestingly, Horace conceptualizes the "antediluvian thighbones" as
leading to a masculine order. "Grandly executed" organizations are predicated on an absence of femininity. The women vanish like dreams, and the
men leave thighbones and ribcages behind—evidence of bodies. In omit-
ting this passage from the published text, Faulkner rescues Horace from
one of his many misconceptions about gender—that the house precludes
femininity—and erases as well the reader's image of the house as overtly
masculine. He also omits the association of men with bodies and women
with dreams, a revision which makes sense in a novel which attests to the
reverse. Finally, he drops an observation which aligns men with grand
culture and women with comfort and happiness, neither of which the
novel supports.

Faulkner's recognition that this house must not be explicitly dissociated
from femininity, as it is from husbandry, supports a reading of space being
gendered as feminine. This gendering, however, does not supply the comfort and happiness which Horace associates with women. As Faulkner
appears to have realized, the feminine space can be perceived as anything
but comfortable. Kristeva, in *Powers of Horror,* identifies both place and
femininity with the abject, a kind of defilement, something that "disturbs
identity, system, order" (4). She describes the "one by whom the abject
exists" as "sounding himself" not in terms of being but "concerning his
place: '*Where* am I?' instead of '*Who* am I?'" (8). This concern with place
can be recast as a concern with the womb, a space which clearly disturbs
identity and order:

> The abject confronts us . . . with our earliest attempts to release the hold of
> *maternal* entity even before ex-isting outside of her, thanks to the autonomy
> of language. It is a violent, clumsy breaking away, with the constant risk of

falling back under the sway of a power as securing as it is stifling. (*Horror* 13)

Thus spaces which seem to evoke the womb are particularly prone to eliciting the abject. Once Narcissa sees the Benbow house as more than a physical place it confronts her with the terror of the abject, with her own defilement.

Figuring place as maternal and abject supports Bleikasten's reading of space as "alien, treacherous, whirling, and dizzying." Place, which functions either as "a threatening outside" or a "suffocating inside" can also represent maternal power, source of home and not-home, self and not-self. Despite the apparent weaknesses of flesh-and-blood mothers, the presence of the maternal resonates throughout the novel. Not the creative power of *Sound and the Fury,* maternity in *Sanctuary* is a destructive force, embodied in structures rather than people. The movement from bodies to buildings allows for a different kind of maternal presence, that of rotting houses rather than the rotting corpse of *As I Lay Dying.* The increased depersonalization of mothering evident in such a shift matches the depersonalization of humanity itself in a novel where characters are described as "a modernist lampstand" (6) and "an effigy on an ancient tomb" (75).

By depriving maternity of a human presence Faulkner goes beyond the maternal absence of *Sound and the Fury* and *As I Lay Dying.* In those texts, the absent center was an absent mother; here not only is the absent mother figured in empty buildings but those empty buildings exude an air of bleakness and abjection which denies the possibility for humanity itself. Narcissa Benbow, trapped in her unconscious association with her childhood home, loses all human compassion for Ruby and goes out of her way to ensure that Horace lose his court case. Because women exist in a world where maternity breeds abjection, virginity breeds weakness, and sexuality breeds contempt, female identity becomes very problematic indeed. The focus on bodies and buildings replaces an examination of psyches, especially for women; much of Horace's agonizing introspection may have been revised out, but his is still the most fully developed psychological profile. In fact, those revisions accomplish more than a de-centering of Horace; they also reflect a de-centering of individual psychology.

The effect of this displaced psychological depth is particularly apparent in Temple Drake. Faulkner carefully avoids an extensive examination of her psyche, thus opening the door to the widely diverse critical responses accorded her.[1] Establishing Temple's character is roughly analogous to solving a detective mystery; one needs to piece together fragments and look for clues in unobvious places. What may be most striking is that her body seems out of touch with her sexuality, as Faulkner repeatedly stresses that she lacks a sexually suggestive figure. Though she is often on the run, which the men clearly find provocative, and there are many scenes of her disrobing, she is also consistently referred to in both childish and boyish terms. Her "arrowlike," "match-thin" body (74) does not suggest feminine voluptuousness and sexuality. Even in her most erotic moments with Red, her sexuality seems horrific rather than passionate, animal rather than human. "When he touched her she sprang like a bow, hurling herself upon him, her mouth gaped and ugly like that of a dying fish as she writhed her loins against him" (252). This exceedingly negative portrayal has led some critics to condemn her nymphomania and others to defend her desperate effort to gain Red's aid in escaping from Popeye. Neither possibility would have been sacrificed, however, had she expressed a more "feminized"— and human—eroticism.

By stripping humanity away from female sexuality, Faulkner strips femininity away as well, possibly implying that sexuality can only be gendered as masculine. While he habitually splits sexuality off from maternity, equally interesting is the way Faulkner's sexually aggressive women— Drusilla Hawk, Joanna Burden, Charlotte Rittenmeyer—invariably take on masculine characteristics. Only Eula Varner, to be discussed later, breaks this pattern. Temple, however, goes significantly beyond these women in her expressed desire to turn into a boy. Judith Butler, in *Gender Trouble,* argues against stable gender identity, asking, "To what extent does the body *come into being* in and through the mark(s) of gender?" (8). Yet Temple's desperate attempt to ward off rape by making the body "come into being" fails because the mark of gender in her case is the mark of sexual difference: the penis. She proceeds through a litany of imaginative fantasies, each designed to obliterate her gender.[2] "I was thinking about if I just was a boy and then I tried to make myself into one by thinking" (227).

When "thinking" fails her, she moves on to seeing herself as a bride in a coffin, yet even there the sound of shucks, symbol of the rape, reaches her: "they had put shucks in the coffin" (230). She then imagines herself a forty-five year old woman with "iron-gray hair and spectacles," but decides "That wont do. I ought to be a man. So I was an old man with a long white beard, and then the little black man got littler and littler and I was saying

Now. You see now. I'm a man now" (230–31). Neither boys nor brides nor gray-haired women carry a powerful enough imaginative wallop to protect her. So Temple turns into "an old man with a long white beard," evoking the unholy pairing of Pap and god, which causes Popeye to get "littler and littler." From Temple's perspective, this final vision succeeds:

> Then I thought about being a man, and as soon as I thought it, it happened. It made a kind of plopping sound, like blowing a little rubber tube wrong-side outward. It felt cold, like the inside of your mouth when you hold it open. I could feel it, and I lay right still to keep from laughing about how surprised he was going to be. (231)

Temple's desperate attempt to believe in this transformation gains sensual support; she both hears and feels it. Her sex change seems complete and successful once it is thus literalized. Possibly in order to protect her protection, she then falls asleep before the hand "got there." What is most outrageous about this outrageous process is that it can be said to work; Temple gets through the night without being physically penetrated. When Horace questions her about her experiences, she speaks only about that night. "That was the only part of the whole experience which appeared to have left any impression on her at all: the night which she had spent in comparative inviolation" (225). Indeed, Temple never narrates directly the actual rape; the interview with Horace ends at the point at which Ruby takes her down to the crib. Thus it remains unclear how much Horace really knows of what happened, whether that bloodstained cob is as much a shock to him as it is to the rest of the courtroom.

Temple's willingness to speak of the night as compared to her reluctance to speak of the rape itself can be understood in many ways. Certainly it makes sense that she should resist speaking of the horror of what she was unable to prevent, and that she might have some pride in her ability to stave off the penetration during the preceeding night. Both incidents constitute sexual assaults, but the second is much more devastating. The first she manages to control—from her persepective—by means of figuration, substantiated by literal sensations. Based on this limited "success," it becomes more easily understandable why she calls on Pap at the point of the second assault. Having found the old man with the white beard a protective device, she again turns to him. This time, however, she does not become a man; she calls on a man. The call proves ineffective, for it is unaided by the literal sensations which reassured her the night before.

Since we never enter Popeye's mind, there is no way of knowing why he
waits until the next morning to complete his assault, other than the possibility that he had no corncob on hand. The importance, however, lies not
in Popeye's reasons but in Faulkner's presentation of the experience. Why
include Temple's fantasies and then delay the rape itself, almost as if in
response to them? I would argue that Temple's use of figuration holds
greater significance than the subject of the fantasy—the desire to erase
one's femininity in the face of sexual abuse. The point is not *what* she
imagines but that she does imagine. Clearly, she is at a physical disadvantage; she has little chance of literally holding off this household of threatening men, and Ruby's aid is tenuous at best.

While she failed to take Ruby's earlier advice to effect her physical
safety by leaving, she relies, as Dianne Luce Cox argues persuasively, on
both Gowan and her class background for protection, not truly believing
that anyone who eats with the governer could be vulnerable to attack. Yet
such protection belongs under the rubric of masculine cultural order, the
Law of the Father, a law which carries no force at the Old Frenchman
place. Once this hope proves false, her only options lie in either the power
of persuasion or in the ability to hide her sex. Given Temple's limited
rhetorical skills, her persuasive efforts fall far short; the best she can come
up with is that the governer dines at their house and that these people are
"just like other people" (59). Language, then, fails her; she cannot persuade
the men to leave her alone, nor does her appeal to Pap bring her any help.
The masculine power of symbolic discourse proves useless, so Temple is
left with the alternative of becoming a man. Where one masculine
mode—language—fails her, another—figuration—appears to grant limited success.

But figuration also fails—precisely because it *is* a figurative and not a
literal transformation. One may "put on" gender; one may not "put on"
sex. For while Temple manages to get through the night in "comparative
inviolation," the worst of her ordeal awaits her. Nowhere in Faulkner's
fiction is feminine power at such a low ebb. Temple cannot negotiate
between the literal and figurative; both fail her in a world controlled not by
the Law of the Father but by paternal outlaws. Because Popeye reigns in
this order, the rules need to be rewritten. Suddenly impotence is strength
and childish fear strikes adults with terror. Tommy's comment about
Popeye, "I be dog if he aint skeered of his own shadow," provokes Horace
to respond, "I'd be scared of it too. . . .If his shadow was mine" (21–22).

Obviously, employing conventional masculine modes will not serve here. Thus, later in her ordeal, Temple takes a different tack, playing up her femininity in her relations with Red. While this tactic has caused numerous critics to heap scorn upon her, it seems the only option left. Yet "putting on" femininity also has its limitations. First of all, it doesn't work. Red does not turn into a white knight and rescue her. Secondly, expressing her sexuality renders her less than human, akin to a dying fish. Rather than constructing a discourse of power through female sexuality, Temple instead discovers that putting on sexuality is as ineffective as putting on gender. Luce Irigaray suggests that to articulate femininity in discourse, the one "path" which has been

> historically assigned to the feminine [is] that of *mimicry*. One must assume the feminine role deliberately. . . .To play with mimesis is thus, for a woman, to try to recover the place of her exploitation by discourse, without allowing herself to be simply reduced to it. It means to resubmit herself— inasmuch as she is on the side of the "perceptible," of "matter"—to "ideas," in particular to ideas about herself, that are elaborated in/by a masculine logic, but so as to make "visible," by an effect of playful repetition, what was supposed to remain invisible: the cover-up of a possible operation of the feminine in language. (76)

Playing with mimesis is never playful in Faulkner; from Drusilla Hawk's attempted seduction of her stepson to Joanna Burden's nymphomania, it is always undertaken by sexually aggressive women and always contains a touch of horror. In submitting to the ideas about women's identity in this culture—that women exist to serve men—Temple makes visible the lack of humanity which masculine culture attempts to cover up. If we read Temple's seductive poses and apparent animalistic desires as the attempt to play on expectations of masculine logic, to make visible the "possible operation of the feminine in language," then the whole situation is capable of an interpretation different from the standard readings of perversion and corruption or even the more sympathetic ones of terror. From this perspective, Temple's behavior becomes a desperate attempt to articulate what she cannot speak verbally—a feminine discourse which will prove effective in the face of male aggression. This play with mimesis reveals female sexuality, the only tool left her, as utterly inadequate. Thus what is made visible is not the feminine in language but the female as victim of men and of her body.

In fact, what Temple makes visible goes beyond the unspeakability of the feminine; it reveals the silencing of humanity itself. The scene with Red, which relies on animal imagery to describe human sexuality, indicates that "playful" exaggeration of sexuality not only reduces Temple to her sexuality but denies any human element to that sexuality. By playing with mimesis, Faulkner illustrates that, in covering up the feminine, masculine logic covers up the human as well. He presents a world which defiles itself when it defiles its women. Having, through her experiences and her attempts to deal with them, plumbed the depths of inhumanity and abjection, Temple's only hope in escaping the violence done to her body is to abjure it, to fall back, once again, to language. Yet this time her language constitutes not protective figurative fantasies but lies, the perversion of the figurative into the untrue.

Temple's perjury is symbolically appropriate, whatever it may say about her character. The courtroom, identified by Duvall as "a male space" (75), breaks down the feminine associations of enclosed spaces. Full of men, the courtroom is the place where one uses language to attain justice. Thus Temple's perjury constitutes her final stand against the masculine world. When women's bodies have been so violently abused, is it any wonder that language, associated with men, should show the strain as well? Temple, whose almost automatic replies clearly suggest that she is simply the mouthpiece of a deal worked out between her father and Popeye, has now been linguistically violated as well. This voice, which differs markedly from the one with which she related her night of comparative inviolation to Horace, has become as inhuman as her sexuality—it is "parrotlike" (300). Caught between body and language, fish and parrots, Temple loses physical form altogether, vanishing into waves of music and the dreary European landscape.

> [S]he seemed to follow with her eyes the waves of music, to dissolve into the dying brasses, across the pool and the opposite semi-circle of trees where at sombre intervals the dead tranquil queens in stained marble mused, and on into the sky laying prone and vanquished in the embrace of the season of rain and death. (333)

This final scene in "the season of rain and death," marks the vanquishing not only of Temple but also of discourse and humanity. Nothing is spoken and nothing is human in the killing "embrace" of the weather. The "embrace," with its clear connotation of sexuality, closes off both the novel and any opportunity for redemption. In what may be his bleakest novel, Faulkner confronts the implications of living in a world where women represent the abject, bodies exist to be defiled, and sexuality leads to inhumanity. Given the emphasis on the body throughout the text, this illustration of its dissolution marks the final defeat of the physical, the mode generally associated with the feminine. It also marks the defeat of humanity and of art. Nothing is created; rather, people and ideals are destroyed in a culture which fails to tap the creative potential of the maternal. *Sanctuary* reveals what transpires when women are either reduced entirely to their sexuality or separated entirely from it. Female sexuality which does not lead to maternity constitutes the threat without the creativity, and both men and women pay the price for its absence.

The Hamlet, unlike *Sanctuary,* is a novel of fertility, a novel, as Joseph Reed says, of "plentitude" (225). "It has," writes Donald Kartiganer, "a status of god-approval, as if touched with holy power" (111). Such terms are never encountered in the critical discourse about *Sanctuary,* where discussions focus not on "holy power" but rather on the power of evil. Additionally, unlike *Sanctuary, The Hamlet,* generally identified as one of Faulkner's best works, has enjoyed a favorable critical reception; scholars praise the poetry, humor, mysticism, and realism of the novel. But amid these admittedly significant distinctions, the two books have a great deal in common. The Old Frenchman's place figures prominently in each. Both privilege social identity and community over individual psychology, distancing the reader from the characters. Both note the inadequacy of the law in establishing justice. Both present maternity and female sexuality as deviant, though mothering plays a more central role in *The Hamlet.* In both novels, women disrupt the masculine cultural order, especially in *The Hamlet,* where they threaten the male bonding and male competition which dominate the action. Finally, both novels examine the interplay between bodies and language, maternal and patriarchal authority in settings which ostensibly impose strict gender divisions.

In *The Hamlet,* however, language figures much more prominently; this is a novel not just of physical plentitude but also of linguistic plentitude. From the narrator's poetic diction to Ab's horse swapping to Ratliff's involved goat-trading machinations to the Texan's persuasive rhetoric, language dominates the characters and the action. Yet, as Louise K. Barnett points out, the world of the novel is a "restricted speech community, an isolated world that paradoxically speaks most eloquently as a spectrum of the inarticulate and unexpressed" (400). She argues that significance lies not so much in the spoken as in the visual: "What is significant in this world is *seen,* not spoken; phenomena of nature, whether Eula Varner or the spotted horses, impact upon the community directly through a physical presence that requires no expression or validation in language" (401).

But if that "physical presence" eschews "expression or validation in language," it nonetheless is controlled by language. While the immediate physicality of "phenomena of nature" such as Eula, the horses, and the cow unquestionably speaks to the power of the literal, to a feminine force almost unknown in *Sanctuary,* the power of discourse—both verbal and silent—reigns supreme. As John Matthews observes, "*The Hamlet* displays a world unalterably established on the discourses of society; there are no natural centers from which to measure the fall into civilization" (164). If there are no natural centers amid this social discourse, there are female bodies which both resist and succumb to such discourse. The tension between language and bodies characterizes the novel and can be recast, to a certain extent, as a tension between masculine and feminine. Certainly critics have been inclined to categorize this novel, more than almost any other, by gender. Kartiganer notes that "Frenchman's Bend remains essentially male in its codes and values" (128), while David Williams argues that the masculine, "once so completely and awesomely subordinate to the feminine, is now destined to ride in fullest ascendency with the 'calm beautiful mask' of woman beside it toward Jefferson" (205). More recently, Dawn Trouard asserts that Eula Varner Snopes, from *The Hamlet* to *The Town,* is "first, last, and foremost [Faulkner's] bitterest illustration of the patriarchal subjugation of women in American culture" (281).

The common thread running throughout these perspectives is the defeat of the feminine. Despite—or because of—the dripping fertility presented within the text, female power is at a low ebb. Eula's body, imprisoned by corsets, becomes Flem's property; the cow is butchered and fed to Ike; the earth itself is mocked and violated in an insane treasure hunt. Eula, of course, stands as the primary symbol of womanhood and maternity, a marked contrast to Temple Drake. But like Temple, she is defined by her body, ogled and drooled over by the men around her. Eula's voluptuousness, however, contrasts with Temple's boyish figure, as does her seeming passivity with Temple's frantic motion. Eula conceives; Temple does not. Eula is married off to the impotent Flem Snopes, and

Temple is imprisoned in a brothel. Given this denigration of women's bodies, it is easy to decide that the women who inhabit them are soundly defeated, particularly in a community which defines women physically. Yet in a novel in which, according to Matthews, the "social organization makes it a kind of text, a system of discourse" (183), one must read bodies as more than containers of humanity; bodies become texts, and women's bodies express a discourse of femininity resistant to masculine control. Language may rule, but bodies put up a strong fight.

Eula, in particular, displays considerable respect for the body which draws men from miles around. She refuses to be "pawed at," preserving a "ruthless chastity" in the midst of eager suitors (128). Despite a life of physical inactivity, she actively protects her body against both verbal and physical violation. When attacked by Labove whispering "his jumble of fragmentary Greek and Latin verse and American-Mississippi obscenity," she knocks him down with "a full-armed blow in the face" (121). Labove's sacred and profane language cannot withstand Eula's uppercut. Then, in what he perceives as the ultimate insult, she does not bother to demand that the men in her family defend her honor. Having successfully defended herself against sexual assault, she needs no male assistance. Trouard suggests that her deadly use of Washington Irving defeats Labove, remarking, "Washington Irving in the mouth of a woman can cause detumescence." But she still refuses to read it as a significant triumph, for in using Irving's words Eula calls upon "this alien language of the fathers," an "appropriated syntax" (285). Yet Trouard errs slightly in assigning Eula's victory to her use of "the only language patriarchy hears." Eula saves herself by knocking down Labove. When she then compares him to Ichabod Crane, the "old headless horseman," she merely adds insult to defeat. Eula may appropriate an alien language, but she relies upon her physical strength. Unlike Temple, she uses the body she has to resist rape; she does not attempt to call a different one into being or to call upon the father for help.

Eula's self-sufficiency may be read in a number of ways. Her ability to protect herself certainly differentiates her from Temple, though Popeye is a more ruthless adversary than Labove. Eula never finds herself in quite such desperate straits. Temple's repeated reassurance to herself—"my father's a judge"—constitutes a linguistic attempt to render herself beyond violation, relying on her belief that judges' daughters don't get raped. She counts on class identification for protection and, when that fails her, attempts to construct another linguistic escape into literal masculinity. She is very well aware of how her father and brothers would view her damaged value should she be subjected to sexual assault, a realization which undoubtedly enhances her terror. Her fear of losing caste contributes to her fear of sexual violence. But Eula, who appears at ease with her body and her sexuality, finds no reason to invoke her father, a far more powerful figure in this community than even Judge Drake in the society of *Sanctuary*. Eula seems to view the assault as directed against her body, not her class or her family position. Since, as we later discover, she doesn't call her out-of-wedlock pregnancy "trouble," it becomes clear that her social position and reputation mean nothing to her, as she refuses to read this attack symbolically. By removing the assault from the realm of the figurative, she defeats it physically. Because Eula refuses to recognize the more figurative and abstract definitions of the realm of the Father, she retains greater power.

This refusal may restrict Eula to her body, but it is a body with power: "Then the body gathered itself into furious and silent resistance" (121). Even the corsets which Jody insists that Eula wear fail to reign in her voluptuous figure; though "stiff and awkward" at first, she eventually learns to walk "without proclaiming the corsets beneath the dresses of silk in which she looked, not like a girl of sixteen dressed like twenty, but a woman of thirty dressed in the garments of her sixteen-year-old sister" (131–32). Most importantly, it is Eula herself who determines her own sexual activity, choosing both partner and time. This choice is apparently sparked by physical violence, by an attack in which she holds off three out of five attackers and comes out unscathed, while McCarron sustains numerous injuries in dealing with the other two. Though her lack of injuries may stem from the men's reluctance to fight with a woman (they try to meet McCarron alone, but he thwarts them), her avid participation in the brawl illustrates a degree of physical assertion previously unencountered in Eula. The initial blood spilled is not hers but his, subtly revising the order of the loss of virginity. Though McCarron is presented as a rake and experienced ladies' man, he bleeds first.

This reversal of bodily functions, of bleeding, carries into and beyond the sexual act itself. Eula continues her physical dominance by supporting McCarron's injured arm which needs to be reset the following day. Afterwards, McCarron is the one who flees while Eula lives on serenely, undisturbed by her pregnancy. "Eula Varner was in what everyone else but her, as it presently appeared, called trouble" (140). Because Eula refuses to label her behavior she apparently avoids the emotional trauma of an out-of-wedlock pregnancy. She averts disgrace by rejecting language, protecting herself against communal disapproval by not reading her physical condition figuratively—or socially. Refusing to participate in social discourse, she manages to keep her body to herself, a technique which heightens her association with the physical. Just as her body dominates her life leading up to her pregnancy, so it dominates her attention now. Her discomfort is physical, not psychological. "Stop shoving me. . . .I don't feel good" (141). Physically and sexually, Eula remains her own person, as undeterred by social stigma as by Labove's desperate attack.

Her physical ascendency, however, seems to be accompanied by mental stagnation. While Eula's "mindlessness" has been exaggerated by critics—with the possible (and admittedly major) exception of her marriage, she appears to get exactly what she wants, a feat not easily accomplished without some exercise of brain power—she certainly shows little overt evidence of significant mental capacity. The damning descriptions provided by both Ratliff and the narrator invariably highlight her limited mentality:

> She might as well still have been a foetus. It was as if only half of her had been born, that mentality and body had somehow become either completely separated or hopelessly involved; that either only one of them had ever emerged, or that one had emerged, itself not accompanied by, but rather pregnant with, the other. (96)

While the narrator leaves open the question of whether mind and body are "either completely separated or hopelessly involved," Eula's response to Labove suggests that mind and body do, in fact, work in conjunction. She appears to separate not necessarily her mind but rather a sense of social conventions; because she does not mind what people say of her, we seem to assume that she has no mind.

Yet the description implies that Eula may be only half-born, with that half—either mind or body—"not accompanied by, but rather pregnant with, the other." While the narrator resists determining whether body or mind contains the other, the metaphor implicitly highlights the body, for pregnancy is a physical state. Furthermore, Eula's body has such a powerful presence that to subordinate body to mind strains one's credulity. Her body is much more likely to carry her mind. Regardless of which constitutes womb and which fetus, the allusion still identifies both as elements of the physical, either a piece of a body or the originating stage of one. Thus figurative mentality is subsumed but not eradicated by the physical body; Eula embodies both.

Still, she is presented as only half human, a barely sentient womb. Such implications call into question the power of the body to create life, and thus Eula's position as the embodiment of fertility, of physical creativity. But read with a different emphasis, the description also illustrates that her birthing ability transcends the human and partakes of the divine, in that she has the potential both to birth others and to complete her own birth, to bear her own mind. Unlike Zeus, who gives birth to Athena from his head, thereby abolishing the need for mothers, Eula, with the capability to bear herself, abolishes the need for fathers and mothers. The potential of the body to birth the mind not only places the mental in a subordinate condition but also indicates that Eula, far from being mindless, has a body made heavy with its mind.

She thus has far greater creative potential than the seemingly asexual Ratliff, the disembodied narrator, or the impotent Flem. The narrative distortion of Eula becomes more understandable, for she denies the typical bifurcation of body and voice. The narrator, with just a voice, a mind, fails to match her artistic capability. As Matthews writes, "she constitutes within herself both signifier and signified, maidenhead and maiden" (199). The merging of signifier and signified renders Eula independent of narrative reconstruction; her character proves a bit too large to fit the language, just as her body proves a bit too excessive to fit into her clothes, just as her maidenhead proves a bit too strong for the men of the community to conquer.

In and of herself, Eula is self-sufficient. She embodies creator and created, mother and fetus, signifier and signified, but she lives in a community which privileges certain kinds of creativity and signification. Swapping, horse trading, and storytelling are the premier activities of the Frenchman's Bend society, all of which rely upon language. The intricate and elaborate schemes by which the men of the community establish precedence are all based on a kind of one-upsmanship which includes misrepresentations, half truths, and lies. Yet amid all these machinations, the same goods keep changing hands. Ab Snopes and Pat Stamper trade and re-trade the same horse, Mrs. Snopes gains custody of her separator by relinquishing the cow, the Old Frenchman's place shifts ownership several times, and the Texas horses move from one owner to another. Nothing is created in all of this activity; things simply move around.

Eula, however, with her creative potential, stands as a serious threat to this order of society. All rules and hierarchy cease when she enters the picture. Even in school, "the class she was in ceased to have either head or foot twenty-four hours after she entered it . . . she would never be at either end of anything in which blood ran. It would have but one point . . . and she would be that point, that center." Simply by existing she disrupts hierarchical order, precisely because she is both signifier and signified, "at once supremely unchaste and inviolable" (115). With her "supreme unchastity" she defeats the men who would violate her by rendering herself already violated and thus inviolable. Embodying this seeming paradox, Eula explodes the categories which her society imposes on women: virgin and whore become one and the same. Faulkner's men spend a great deal of time trying to separate virginity and maternity, chastity and violation. Eula's erasure of those boundaries makes her possibly one of Faulkner's most threatening women, a woman who resists both physical and verbal restraints, untroubled by either corsets or gossip.

The men of the community seem well aware of her threat. Karen R. Sass, drawing on Nancy Chodorow's work, suggests that these men displace their fear of maternity onto sexuality: these "males cope with the relation to the mother by repressing the primary unity with her and converting it into sexual terms which are then expressed with other women" (129). If they feel for Eula a displaced yearning for the mother, this may explain their mixed feelings of desire and fear toward her. Labove realizes that his feelings for her stem not from "rage at all but terror" (117), and Ratliff sees her as a "mortal natural enemy of the masculine race" (149). Even the boys and men who swarm around express both rage and longing. Interestingly, none of them want to marry her, to procreate legally, possibly due to the maternal association Sass postulates, for to marry her is to legitimize incestuous desires. They simply want to violate her, to destroy her transcendent equilibrium and supreme unchastity.

This overwhelming desire to erase Eula's virginity without legalizing her body through marriage suggests that they want to turn her into an outlaw in order to expel her and cleanse themselves and their community of her disruptive presence. But Eula's own indifference to law and language render this an extremely difficult task, particularly given the nature of the men who attempt it. In trying to control her behavior, they reveal their own impotence. They cannot wash away Eula; the full extent of feminine power is revealed in the inability of the masculine to expel it. "Femininity,"

Shoshana Felman writes, "is neither a metonymy, a snug container of masculinity, nor is it a metaphor—its specular reflection. Femininity *inhabits* masculinity, inhabits [it] as otherness, as its own *disruption*" (42). As both *The Hamlet* and *Sanctuary* illustrate, to eradicate or restrain femininity is to eradicate humanity. Masculinity cannot erase femininity without erasing itself.

Thus Eula becomes an agent of the uncanny, threatening castration and even annihilation to those who gaze upon her. By forcing the men of the community to confront the fragility of their masculinity, she exposes the precariousness of identity itself. In the words of Mary Jacobus, "The monster in the text is not woman, or the woman writer; rather, it is this repressed vacillation of gender or the instability of identity—the ambiguity of subjectivity itself which returns to wreak havoc on consciousness, on hierarchy, and on unitary schemes designed to repress the otherness of femininity" (5). Jody and Labove, who try "to repress the otherness of femininity," Jody by corsets and Labove' by rape, must acknowledge, in their failures, the instability of their masculine identities. Their failure to assert masculinity emblemizes a greater failure to assert self, and thus they lose sexuality, identity, and even being.

Jody, "the apotheosis of the masculine Singular" (7), who emanates "a quality of invincible and inviolable bachelordom" (6), finds himself unable to match Eula's sexuality with his own and is reduced to a "jealous seething eunuch priest" (114). His attempts to make Eula conform to what he considers acceptable female behavior largely focus on efforts to erase her female body. He insists that she attend school, despite her mother's contention that "the proper combining of food ingredients lay not on any printed page but in the taste of the stirring spoon, and that the housewife who had to wait until she had been to school to know how much money she had left after subtracting from it what she had spent, would never be a housewife" (97). Her father only wants "to keep her out of trouble until she gets old enough to sleep with a man without getting me and him both arrested" (98). Jody's determination that Eula get an education seems to mark him as more sympathetic and progressive than his parents, who conceive of Eula's future only in stereotypic terms, as a housewife and sexual object. His emergence as "erudition's champion" stands up even in the face of the humiliations and frustrations he endures to send her to school, as he remains convinced "of the necessity of that for which he now paid so dear a price" (97).

It is a curious conviction, particularly given Eula's apparent indifference to education. Jody gives no reasons for his stand, though he appears to cherish a hope that school will educate Eula away from sexuality. He is clearly embarrassed by Eula's body, and attempts to restrain it through corsets and learning. One could also suggest a motive of sexual jealousy in this attempt to establish education rather than sexuality as defining identity. Jody, the "jealous seething eunuch priest," lacks the sexual charisma which Eula possesses in abundance. His body is mocked, not idolized, as his father taunts him over his weight. "You have just about already got to where you cant get [your head] far enough down to lace your own shoes" (143). The excess which in Eula becomes fertility in Jody turns to obesity. Given his sexual and physical failure, he must privilege mental prowess or admit his own inferiority to his sister. Thus Jody desperately insists on education for Eula in a futile attempt to establish control and gain ascendency, a need which becomes stronger once Flem arrives on the scene and essentially usurps Jody's position as Will's heir. Jody's final exercise of power lies in his attempt to shape Eula, both physically and mentally, a battle in which he has neither the wits nor the body to prevail, and so is reduced to empty words and threats. Stripped of his identity as a son and a brother he becomes a notperson, part of the motley crowd rather than a mighty Varner.

In his notpersonhood, Jody cannot even recognize Eula's pregnancy after spending years guarding against the possibility.

> It was not the father and not even the brother, who for five or six years now had actually been supported upright and intact in breathing life by an idea which had not even grown through the stage of suspicion at all but had sprung fullblown as a conviction only the more violent for the fact that the most unremitting effort had never been able to prove it, whom divination descended upon. (139)

It is the mother, of course, who recognizes impending motherhood. Jody's conviction regarding Eula's imminent pregnancy, which springs "fullblown" rather than growing through stages, recalls Athena's birth out of Zeus's head, an analogy that cannot be dismissed in a novel teeming with mythic imagery. This conviction displaces natural maternal creativity for divine immediacy; the mother gives way to Zeus (who, of course, had swallowed her in order to usurp her creative power). But the idea thus conceived is at first unprovable and then ultimately unrecognizable. In trying to sidestep gradual development, a process which mirrors pregnancy, Jody fails to bring to birth any idea at all. His inability to read the body, even the body on which he keeps such a close watch, and his reliance on full-blown rather than developing ideas, renders him utterly incompetent to deal with Eula.

Upon learning of her pregnancy he demands that she speak, that she name the father of her child. She simply ignores him, refusing even to refuse to answer, a response which infuriates him possibly because it denies the role of symbolic discourse in dealing with the situation. Consequently, he can only think of going after her most recent suitors and finding someone—a man—who will use language and thus cast the situation into a realm he can handle. "By God . . . maybe she wont talk but I reckon I can find somebody that will" (143). He seeks desperately after legitimacy, the only tool left him to identify, categorize, and thus control the fate of Eula's body. But since Eula does not accept social or legal conventions as guiding or defining principles, she vanquishes Jody without a fight by refusing to recognize his terms or his weapon, namely, language. He is left sputtering meaningless words, utterly unable to exert either his verbal or physical dominance, essentially castrated and even deposed of his identity. From this point on Jody vanishes from the novel, save for a few casual references. Not just his masculinity but his very being is eradicated.

Labove, another would-be shaper of Eula's destiny, shares Jody's sexual impotence. A man whose face displays an "invincible conviction in the power of words as a principle worth dying for," a face which, a thousand years ago, "would have been a monk's" (105), he also finds himself ignominiously defeated by Eula. In contrast to Jody, he sees immediately that "there was nothing in books here or anywhere else that she would ever need to know, who had been born already completely equipped not only to face and combat but to overcome anything the future could invent to meet her with" (114). Because he determines this based on his first glimpse of Eula, Labove is clearly reacting to her body, deciding that anyone with her physical attributes is already "equipped" to face life. While Jody appears to cherish a hope that learning will de-sexualize her, Labove views her in exclusively sexual terms, as beneath and beyond books. This probably accounts for his rage and humiliation when he realizes that she has, in fact, managed to imbibe at least some knowledge as she taunts him with deadly literary accuracy.

Interestingly, Labove, with his reverence for words and his law degree, feels no desire to marry Eula, to legalize a union and thus to bring Eula back into the realm of law, for she carries more appeal to the outlaw in him. Thus, despite his passion, "he did not want her as a wife, he just wanted her one time as a man with a gangrened hand or foot thirsts after the axe-stroke which will leave him comparatively whole again" (118). His association of sexual intercourse with amputation reveals vividly his revulsion against sexuality and his castration fears; yet he persists in thinking of her only in sexual terms, thus trapping himself precisely in the realm which most threatens him. He does, however, attempt to reconceptualize his own sexual violence and potency in discursive terms, wanting "to leave some indelible mark of himself on [Eula's face] and then watch it even cease to be a face" (119). He may want to inscribe himself upon her, but she is the one who inscribes him, striking him down with "a full-armed blow in the face" (121), refusing to allow her body to become a text for his "indelible mark."

Just as she denies Jody the position of avenger, so she refuses Labove even the vicarious fulfillment of fighting Jody and thus achieving "an orgasm of sorts, a katharsis, anyway—something" (122). He disappears from Frenchman's Bend, unable to cope with his impotence, and, even more importantly, with his insignificance. "She never told him at all. She didn't even forget to. She doesn't even know anything happened that was worth mentioning" (126). Like Jody, Labove is defeated by Eula's refusal to use language, a refusal which imprisons him in the physical realm where he has just been so decisively defeated, and denies him the opportunity to attempt to redeem his body by substituting physical prowess for sexual potency. Having suffered such a complete linguistic and bodily defeat, he has no choice but to take his body out of town.

It is Will Varner, the father, who manages to control Eula's fate. He scoffs at Jody's demand for ultimate legitimacy, realizing that her erstwhile suitors are halfway to Texas. Will, a man of vast sexual experience, seems less disturbed at Eula's pregnancy than Jody; bodies are there to be used. "What did you expect—that she would spend the rest of her life just running water through it?" (144). Because he is not personally affronted or threatened by her sexuality, he is able to operate with his wits rather than with Jody's blind rage or Labove's blind passion. Yet Will recognizes the importance of legitimacy as much as Jody, and he is considerably more skilled in attaining it. He is less concerned with finding the "right" father than with finding a legal husband. Rather than wasting time with words,

Will acts, marrying Eula off to Flem Snopes. Where other men fail to control Eula's fate, the father and the law succeed.

It is surely no accident that Will Varner, the sexually active father, wields the greatest power, for he literally imposes the law. Will says little directly; his manipulations take place behind the scenes and are only illuminated through recorded documents: marriage licenses and deed transfers. Thus Will combines considerable sexual experience and human understanding with a canny realization of the power of the law to carry out his schemes. Verbal discourse—Jody's blustering and Labove's "jumble of fragmentary Greek and Latin verse and American-Mississippi obscenity"— lacks the force of written legal documents, the kind of power which, apparently, only a father holds; Will is a Justice of the Peace like the other Justice who judges the two actions in "The Peasants," "a neat, small, plump old man resembling a tender caricature of all grandfathers who ever breathed" (323). He may be a grandfatherly caricature, but he holds the paternal power of the law.

When confronted with the power of the text and the law, Eula is basically denied her body, described now by what covers her rather than what lies beneath the covers, becoming the signified rather than the signifier. She goes to her wedding wearing a "calm beautiful mask . . . beneath the Sunday hat, the veil, above the Sunday dress, even the winter coat." Her once-powerful body has now become a mannequin. Having reduced Eula to her garments, the narrator comments on Flem beside her, carrying his "straw suitcase on his knees like the coffin of a baby's funeral" (145). The reference to a baby's coffin is apt in that presenting the unborn child with Flem Snopes for a father constitutes a kind of murder, but the simile extends further. By invoking a baby's funeral, Faulkner also invokes the death of physical creativity. Stifled by paternal law, maternity loses force as Eula is reduced from goddess to nearly illegitimate mother, from idol to object. Despite her beauty, strength, and power, she is defeated by the forces of her father, by the language on the legal document which transfers her to Flem's custody. Will Varner's greeting to the townspeople may be "perfectly inflectionless, unreadable" (145), but everyone can read the words on the marriage license which he has bought. Even Eula's body is no match for the language of the marketplace and the law. In a linguistically determined world, one needs the Father's language to compete. Her resistance to language may allow her to triumph over the likes of Jody and Labove, but it cannot help her defeat the Father, the ruler of symbolic discourse.

Eula is even less articulate than Temple, uttering, to my count, eleven sentences (including fragments) in the whole novel. Of course, one need only recall Jody or Labove to remember that talking does not necessarily confer power in *The Hamlet,* but Eula's silence seems excessive given her importance to the community and the novel, and the significance which is placed upon the power of speech. A lot of talking goes on in Frenchman's Bend, but virtually none of it comes from women. Eula says little, her mother says less, and Mrs. Littlejohn's few cogent remarks are largely ignored by men intent on being defrauded. Both Mrs. Armstid and Mrs. Tull speak, but to little avail. Lucy Pate apparently never speaks directly to Jack Houston during the years when she does his homework for him, and Mink Snopes's wife, the one exception, a woman who expresses herself freely, relies more on the use of her body than the use of her voice.

Thus Eula has no models of successful women's speech. Given that women speak only to be ignored, she at least spares herself the ignominy of useless verbiage. She refuses to play a game in which the deck is stacked against her. But her refusal also constitutes a defeat, for by remaining silent she leaves herself open to the defining voices of Ratliff and the narrator. While her silence certainly renders her vulnerable to narrative violation, to be discussed shortly, even more serious is her defeat by written documents. Talk is negligible; writing is not. The marriage license seals Eula's fate and her body. The woman who appears in *The Town* embarks on a career of desperation in contrast to the serenity she evokes and the power she exercises in *The Hamlet.*

Given the constraint it imposes on her, Eula's acquiescence to this marriage bears scrutiny, particularly in light of her previous strength and imperviousness to others' attempts to control her. Why would the girl who shows no interest in dolls or toy stoves, who takes no active role in adolescent courting, and who apparently has no concern over an out-of-wedlock pregnancy agree to marry Flem Snopes? Obviously Will Varner orchestrates the marriage, but Eula still has to agree and, given her general inertness, one can easily imagine her simply ignoring her father's demands. While Eula does, on occasion, show distinct signs of exerting her will in refusing to walk, defending herself against Labove, and engaging in sexual intercourse with McCarron, in this matter she appears volitionless. "And so one day they clapped her into her Sunday clothes . . . and took her to town in the surrey and married her to him" (146–47). The narrative suggests a kind of fatality in the events, a forthcoming doom which Eula herself recognizes. "It was as if she really knew what instant, moment, she was reserved for, even if not his name and face, and was waiting for that moment rather than merely for the time for the eating to start, as she seemed to be" (128). Yet this fatalistic passivity does not mesh with Eula's sexual initiative with McCarron. Attributing a kind of doom to her life may help to exonerate her of the poor judgment in accepting Flem, but it robs her of any will or responsibility.

The only comment on her possible feelings for Flem is that she "knew him well" (145). Knowledge is not generally associated with Eula. Labove decides that there is nothing she needs to know because she is "completely equipped" to face life; in school she answers either "I dont know" or "I never got that far" (114). Apparently, however, she knows Flem well, but her knowledge is of a curious type. She knows him "so well that she never had to look at him anymore" (145). The need to see him vanishes once he moves into the house with them. Eula's knowledge must be instinctual, a kind of Faulknerian notknowledge. As soon as he becomes a part of the domestic scene, a scene in which Eula has never expressed any interest except to eat the food prepared and to move out of the way of cleaning, he ceases to exist as a visual object. As a part of the household she may ignore him or she may marry him; if the latter, he remains equally meaningless to her. Because she cares nothing about legality and social convention, a husband, any husband, is simply an extraneous appendage, a different kind of corset which may or may not succeed in confining her body. Eula's tragedy, as Ratliff notes, is not that she marries Flem Snopes. It is that she is a fertile creative woman in a world where women are feared and com-modified.

Eula appears to exert herself only to get pregnant; once she achieves this goal, nothing else matters. Yet becoming a mother does not grant her the power of Caddy Compson or Addie Bundren. Indeed, once violated, she loses stature. This community respects the power not of maternity but only of potential maternity, fertility as yet unfulfilled. The feminine threat lies in sexuality unpossessed by men. Once legalized, female sexuality loses a great deal of its appeal. Law controls women's bodies more effectively than men can, possibly explaining its centrality in the community. In *The Hamlet* law shows as little justice towards women as it does in *Sanctuary*.

Legal discourse, the one mode which appears to have power over Eula, has no effect at all on her husband. Matthews has brilliantly illustrated the limitations of the law with respect to controlling Flem. The judge is defeated by "Flem's refusal to recognize the court's papers and by Lump's cheerful perjury. Snopesism reflects the dangerous properties of civilization, which depends on the condition of writing (through its spoken words, contracts, laws, and documents)" (Matthews 190). Likewise, in Ratliff's imagined scenario, Flem, a man of little speech, masterfully outdevils Satan by calling upon his legal written rights. *"He says he dont want no more and no less than his legal interest according to what the banking and civil laws states in black and white is hisn"* (150). Law, based on written contractual agreements, rarely dispenses justice. But the chief victims of the law are neither the men who foolishly buy the spotted horses despite the evidence of their eyes as to the horses' worth, nor Mink Snopes, who takes the law into his own hands and then is betrayed by Flem's refusal to come to his defense. The chief victims are women. As inadequate as the law may be in regulating men's behavior, it imposes a tight rein on women.

Mrs. Tull, indeed, fully recognizes this as she sits in the courtroom with "an outrage which curiously and almost at once began to give the impression of being directed not at any Snopes or at any other man in particular but at all men, all males, and of which Tull himself was not at all the victim but the subject" (323). She knows that she has been victimized by Flem Snopes, her husband, the horses which are obvious male symbols, the men who bought them, and now, the Justice and the law. Tull, though he has sustained considerable injuries in the accident, would clearly never have brought suit, as his wife realizes.

> You'll let Eck Snopes or Flem Snopes or that whole Varner tribe snatch you out of the wagon and beat you half to death against a wooden bridge. But when it comes to suing them for your just rights and a punishment, oh no. Because that wouldn't be neighborly. What's neighborly got to do with you lying flat on your back in the middle of planting time while we pick splinters out of your face? (328)

The code of neighborliness does not apply to women, who will have to pay the price of Tull's forbearance. Masculine ethics fails to take women's concerns into account. Mrs. Tull, who has the most at stake in this lawsuit since she will have to cover what Tull can no longer perform, thus comes out the biggest loser. Ironically, even though Eck Snopes is willing to accept responsibility for the horse, the law protects him: "In the law, ownership cant be conferred or invested by word-of-mouth. It must be established either by recorded or authentic document, or by possession or occupation" (330). Speech does not confer legality, and Mrs. Tull, who has only words to prove her case, is awarded the horse, the emblem of everything which has conspired against her. Somehow, there is enough legal authority to ensure that women can attain no satisfaction from the law, even when individual men are willing to settle. The masculine power of the law transcends that of fair-minded men.

Mrs. Armstid, a woman more beaten down, is an even more tragic victim. She too acts on her own to try to settle her grievance, since her husband, who completed the transaction against her will, would never attempt to deny its validity. Indeed, her case rests largely on her husband's insanity, a claim which even the Texan respects. Though each woman's attitude is presented differently, Mrs. Armstid goes to court with the same lack of belief in justice. While Mrs. Tull's sense of futility comes across in her hostility to men and the male system, Mrs. Armstid reveals a marked indifference to telling the story: "She told it, unmoving, in the flat, inflectionless voice, looking at nothing, while they listened quietly, coming to the end and ceasing without even any fall of voice, as though the tale mattered nothing and came to nothing" (325). Will Varner's "inflectionless" greeting to his neighbors at the time of Eula's marriage belies his shrewd machinations; Mrs. Armstid's "inflectionless voice" illustrates her realization that she cannot possibly win a case against Flem Snopes. One voice hides success, and the other reveals failure. The tale does, indeed, matter nothing, for tales abound in this book. Lump Snopes caps Mrs. Armstid's story with a better one—or, at least, with a legally enforceable one.

In Mrs. Tull's case, word-of-mouth evidence lacks authority, despite its obvious truth; in Mrs. Armstid's, it determines the outcome, despite its obvious falsity. Understanding that words, as Addie Bundren says, are "no good" to her, Mrs. Armstid attempts to shift the emphasis to things, to the literal, so often women's strong suit. She announces that she would recognize the bills and coins themselves. "I earned that money a little at a time and I would know it when I saw it because I would take the can outen the chimney and count it now and then while it was making up to enough to buy my chaps some shoes for next winter. I would know it if I was to see it again" (326). This constitutes a shrewd move on her part, looking to change the terms of the suit from words to physical evidence. But such a shift, which might privilege women's ways of knowing, cannot be allowed in a male court of law. Lump's perjury carries more weight. Mrs. Armstid gains only a "little sweetening for the chaps" (317), a five-cent bag of candy from Flem, a bitter mockery of her attempt to make physical things count as much as spoken words. Her response, "You're right kind," may reveal an ironic recognition of the power of verbal speech—her words here carry the same weight as her words in court—but it is poor consolation for the loss of the money she worked so hard to acquire.

Women cannot hope to gain redress with or against words. Not only are their actions and bodies subject to the male characters' words, but their very identities are contolled by the narrative perspective of the book. Though Eula prevents her body from becoming a text for Labove's "indelible mark," she remains vulnerable to narrative's ability to write her body. While both Ratliff and the narrator seem to present a neutral and omniscient view of Eula, it gradually becomes clear that the men narrating Eula do her at least as much violence as those attacking her. What Trouard writes of Eula in *The Town* is equally true here: she "is frozen in and by male discourse" (284). It is worth examining the nature of that male discourse, to see from what position Eula is defined and judged.

With his "hearty celibacy" (42), his compassion for Ike, and his considerable abilities as a storyteller and trader, Ratliff has gained nearly universal approbation from critics, despite the greed which leads to his defeat at Flem's hands and despite his identification of Eula as "just meat, just galmeat" (149).[3] Faulkner takes great pains to establish Ratliff as an almost androgynous figure, equally at home swapping tales and goods with men and "among the women surrounded by laden clotheslines and tubs and blackened wash pots beside springs and wells" (13). With "an air of perpetual bachelorhood," he comes across as asexual, a man distanced from most of the folly which characterizes the rest of the male population of Frenchman's Bend (42). Though Ratliff often sounds similar to the disembodied unidentified narrator, he is more than a voice. He, too, has a body, one which draws considerable attention when violated by the surgeon's knife. That Faulkner adds this seemingly unnecessary detail regarding Ratliff demands attention. If the operation gives him a new lease on life, he fails to take full advantage of the opportunity, finding himself unable to predict the end of his goat-trading scheme. "It was because I have been sick, was slowed up, that I didn't—" (85).

While Ratliff himself feels that his operation has primarily affected his brains and understanding (and his pocketbook), the narrative descriptions of him focus on his body:

> So he sat, thin, the fresh clean blue shirt quite loose upon him now, yet looking actually quite well, the smooth brown of his face not pallid but merely a few shades lighter, cleaner-looking; emanating in fact a sort of delicate robustness like some hardy odorless infrequent woodland plant blooming into the actual heel of winter's snow, nursing his coffee cup in one thin hand. (68)

The bodily weakness which apparently contributes to the mental weakness (at least, weakness when compared to his adversary) is interestingly underscored by the references to cleanliness, which would also render him at a considerable disadvantage when dealing with Flem Snopes. With his "cleaner-looking" face and thin hands, Ratliff finds his body unequal to his goal, marking a clear connection between physical and mental capability. One needs physical strength to wage a psychological war.

Yet if his illness works as an excuse here, the same can hardly be said of his ignominious defeat in a salted mine. While bodily deformity is highlighted in the disastrous treasure hunt, the body in question is Henry Armstid's, not Ratliff's. Ratliff, in fact, spends much of his time restraining Armstid's "furious body" (339). In this episode he has his own body under control but still falls prey to Flem's machinations. Louise Barnett suggests that this failure results from Ratliff's "mistaken assumption that Will Varner lied about the property's lack of value." Because Ratliff privileges the gamesmanship of barter and verbal manipulation above the possibility of simple truth, he becomes as much a victim of "a fiction of his own making as by the machinations of a trickster" (404).

Certainly Ratliff succumbs to his own elaborate fictions, yet he also drives himself into physical exhaustion, thus dulling his senses, and then ignores physical warnings emanating from those senses. When he sees Eustace Grimm on the gallery of the store, he believes that, sharpened by his exhaustion, he has put everything together:

> Maybe sleeping rests a man, but it takes staying up all night for two or three nights and being worried and scared half to death during them, to sharpen him. Because as soon as he recognised Grimm, something in him had clicked, though it would be three days before he would know what it was. He had not had his clothes off in more than sixty hours; he had had no breakfast today and what eating he had done in the last two days had been more than spotty—all of which showed in his face. But it didn't show in his voice or anywhere else, and nothing else but that showed anywhere at all. (349)

Ratliff's exhaustion may not show in his voice, but it shows physically, possibly giving him away. Ratliff's voice, after all, does not fail him; his senses do. Because it takes him three days (very likely due to his physical condition) to realize what had "clicked"—the question of Eustace Grimm's family connections—he fails to act upon the subconscious warning. By ignoring the clicking, which Faulkner presents as an actual physical action, and relying upon his voice rather than listening to his body, Ratliff loses the game, his loss a function of the body as much as the mind.

Interestingly, rather than feeling sympathy for Eula in recognizing the power of the physical, Ratliff denies this potential tie. While Jody tries to reduce Eula's sexuality, possibly as a response to his own lack in that capacity, Ratliff tries to reduce her mental capacity, possibly to distance himself further from his own physical weakness by highlighting the dehumanizing effect of her body. He displaces his own unacknowledged vulnerability to the physical onto Eula and further challenges any possible relation to himself by linking it to her gender. Dismissing her—and thus her tragedy—as "just gal-meat," and noting that "there was a plenty of that, yesterday and tomorrow too" (149) indicates a surprising callousness to her fate, particularly striking from the man who shows such compassion for Ike, refusing to profit at his expense.

Eula, however, is a woman, a sexual being, and thus of a species even further removed from his own than the mentally deficient Ike Snopes. Consequently, his concern is not for Eula herself but for "the waste, not wasted on Snopes but on all of them, himself included—Except was it waste?" While he initially identifies himself as one of those who have proved unworthy of Eula's potential, he backs away from this conclusion, apparently deciding that the problem may lie with Eula rather than "all of them."

> He looked at the face again. It had not been tragic, and now it was not even damned, since from behind it there looked out only another mortal natural enemy of the masculine race. And beautiful: but then, so did the highwayman's daggers and pistols make a pretty shine on him; and now as he watched, the lost calm face vanished. (149)

Because Eula is a woman, "only another mortal natural enemy of the masculine race," she cannot be damned. This identification of Eula as undamnable denies her human identity as surely as Temple Drake is dehumanized through the animal imagery associated with her. Even Eula's

beauty becomes deadly, taking on the shine of "the highwayman's daggers
and pistols." This beauty is not just destructive; it is phallic. While less
explicitly presented than Drusilla Hawk's fondling of the dueling pistols in
The Unvanquished, the reference to daggers and pistols here evokes a
phallic power which Ratliff is quick to erase. Once he makes the connection between Eula and the highwayman's weapons, she disappears: "the
lost calm face vanished." Unwilling to contemplate the possibility of Eula
as powerful—even deadly—Ratliff quickly defuses the force of his analogy by limiting it to the "pretty shine" of the weapons. Focusing on the
surface reduces the threat of the daggers and pistols as well as that of the
woman's body by evoking her mask rather than her sexuality. Trivialized
from tragic to damned to simply lost, Eula vanishes altogether, much like
Temple who "dissolves" at the close of *Sanctuary.* From this point on, Eula
ceases to play a significant role in the novel, replaced as a symbol of
feminine abundance by a cow. Ike Snopes may have "thick female thighs"
(171) and the cow may represent "the flowing immemorial female" (165),
but to transfer the feminine power which Eula embodies to this grotesque
love story marks the degree to which the dehumanization of the feminine
has progressed.

How are we to read this triumph of male narrative authority? The
phallic imagery applied to Eula not only erases her from the narrative, it
also erases human female sexuality. But Eula essentially disappears even
earlier, possibly at the point at which she marries Flem, when she enters
into a legal contract regarding the dispensation of her body. In fact,
Matthews argues that there may be nothing to disappear: Eula "is no mere
exaggeration of the unspeakable pleasures of the erotic virgin. . . .Rather,
she embodies the paradox that what seems an immediate, full presence has
already been marked as 'lost' by its articulation." Once Eula "finds her way
into the world (and the narrative)," he continues, "her purity becomes a
kind of foulness, her virginity a sexual violation, her fullness a bursting"
(198).

The ways in which the narrative articulates Eula unquestionably mark
her as already "lost," yet that loss presumes a kind of feminine origin, a
platonic female essence of which she is the inadequate representative, the
deferred sign. All the mythic imagery associated with Eula enhances her
status as a goddess, a divinity, a more-than-woman. The product of a
"spendthrift Olympian ejaculation" (147), she is larger than life, emanating

"that outrageous quality of being, existing, actually on the outside of the garments she wore" (101). Matthews suggests that this "overstatement of her body reminds us that Eula is a figure of speech" (200). I would argue, however, that while Eula's body calls attention to its fictionality as a narrative construct, it is not so easy to dismiss the implications of the physicality narrated.

If Eula is simply the trace of an "immediate, full presence," she is also the trace of the uncanny site of feminine origin, the womb. The desperate need to vanquish her, to render her a figure of speech rather than a procreative body, reveals the need of the masculine culture to reimpose the economic and patriarchal system on which the community rests. Jacobus writes, "Hysteria, women, and the uncanny are the points of instability which threaten to expose theory, sexual difference, and 'reality' as themselves the product of representation; as constructs" (201). By exposing "reality" as "construct," Eula's evocation of female origin uncovers the degree to which Frenchman's Bend is a figure of speech, highlights the fictionality of masculinity, and challenges the barter system on which the social discourse is grounded.

Eula, far from serving as an exchangeable commodity, actually explodes the economics of Frenchman's Bend. Instead of auctioning off his daughter as a prize to the highest bidder, Will Varner must pay Flem to take her off his hands. While Will once hoped that she could find a husband "that will keep Jody out of the poorhouse too" (98), now that she has become damaged goods she turns into a liability rather than an asset. Not only must Will sign away the Old Frenchman's place, a piece of property which apparently has considerable personal value for him, he also cashes a $300 check, presumably as a further inducement to Flem, and even pays for the marriage license. As Luce Irigaray points out, virgins are "*pure exchange value*" (186), but "mothers cannot circulate in the form of commodities without threatening the very existence of the social order" (185). Eula's very existence has frayed the social order enough; Will cannot risk waiting until she actually becomes a mother, at which point financial loss is subsumed in social anarchy. Thus he offers her for free, with land and $300 thrown in, trying to cut his losses before they overwhelm this world over which he reigns.

In fact, social anarchy has already occurred. The debasement of Eula's exchange value leads structurally to the debasement of women's sexuality to the bestial, as Ike's love affair with the cow replaces Eula in the text. The very outrageousness of this situation, however, calls attention to its own fictionality, just as Eula's excessive body invokes similar questions. Matthews may argue that Eula is "no mere exaggeration," but exaggeration she certainly is. The abundance and excess of this novel can be considered as a possible play with mimesis, as feminine sexuality is made all too visible. Despite the fact that they ultimately become cogs in the economic structure of the community, held in thrall by the Snopeses, women have demonstrated their uncanny ability to jam the masculine machinery by calling into question, through what Irigaray calls their "*disruptive excess*" (78), sexuality and identity as stable constructs.

The "disruptive excess" of femininity in this novel, whether it be Eula, the cow, or the atmosphere of mythic fertility, may be tamed by the end, reabsorbed into the "univocal" discourse of Snopesism, but the cost has been considerable. In an ironic revision of the myth of Zeus and Europa, a divinity is transformed into a cow not for the purposes of sexual consummation and procreation, but precisely to contain such potential. Structurally, this maneuver succeeds; imaginatively, it fails. The narrative effectively displaces Eula, who is not even mentioned in the final scene of Flem's triumph, as he watches Henry Armstid's mad treasure hunt. The new object of the communal gaze, Armstid takes over Eula's position. An even more tragic victim than Eula herself, he reveals the truth of Ratliff's realization that Eula's fate reflects the failure of the entire community, the price one must pay for substituting economics for humanity.

Women are robbed of their sexual power and men are robbed of their sanity. It is "as though," Ratliff muses, "the gods themselves had funnelled all the concentrated bright wet-slanted unparadised June onto a dung-heap, breeding pismires" (159–60). The association of fertility with a dung-heap invokes the power of the abject, that force which causes one to question the boundaries of human existence. Ultimately, Faulkner reveals the de-humanization of humanity which results from the denigration and de-sexualization of women. As Felman observed, "femininity inhabits masculinity." The men who attack it, confine it, or barter it do so not only at their own peril but at the peril of society. It surely is no accident that the novel most teeming with female fertility is also the one which documents the rise of the forces of emotionless economics. As in *Sanctuary*, the defeat of women's sexuality reveals the emptiness of the social order. Wasting creative potential, be it literal or figurative, is a crime against art and humanity, punished by the triumph of the Snopeses.

The Hamlet, like *Sanctuary,* deals with the ways that female sexuality threatens the male-dominated cultural order. Amid the power of the law and language, women's bodies, whether as idolized as Eula's or as dese-crated as Temple's, once again provide the feminine excess which jams the machinery of patriarchal society. Largely excluded from symbolic dis-course and surrounded by impotent men, both women uncover the frag-ility of masculinity and of its defining hold over human identity. Women's bodies evoke the reminder of the mother's physical originating power, a force which is only violated at the cost of humanity itself.

Chapter 4

Bodies and Language

Light in August and *The Wild Palms*

*L*ight in August* and *The Wild Palms* reflect a different perspective on maternal power in that they contain mothers who are both living and present. In marked contrast to *Sanctuary* and *The Hamlet,* these two novels examine women's considerable facility in the literal as well as the figurative realms. Babies are born, language is spoken, and men struggle to understand women who function both sexually and maternally. Probably Faulkner's closest approximations to love stories, the books examine the relationships between men and women in great detail. But invariably, love flounders in the gap between men's and women's language or is devastatingly challenged by the complications of female procreative power. While the women presented meet a variety of fates, few of them pleasant, their creative use of bodies and language reflect Faulkner's growing realization of the possibilities embodied in maternal power and discourse. Breaking down boundaries of race and gender, these books attest to the creative power derived from maternal fluidity, despite the cost it can exact from both men and women.

When Byron Bunch hears Lena Grove's "moaning wail" during childbirth, he realizes that she seems "to be speaking clearly to something in a tongue which he knew was not his tongue nor that of any man" (399). Women's language in *Light in August* may be clearly spoken, but it is expressed in a tongue unknown to men, providing an alternative to the male symbolic discourse which appears to control the fictional world. This time, however, it is men, not women, who are excluded, for Joe Christmas as well as Byron experiences language as alien, as defining a world in which he does not belong. Symbolic discourse, traditionally the vehicle of the Father, is thus challenged as the defining characteristic of masculinity. Despite André Bleikasten's assertion, "With Faulkner, the Father—especially the Dead Father—is always the one who names, places, marks, the one who casts the spell, whether through his voice or his eyes" (87), in *Light in August* Faulkner also testifies to a counterforce embodied in Lena's unknown tongue, which can be viewed as a maternal alternative to the traditionally male "mastery" of language. His women characters evade the boundaries and categories by which the men attempt to control them. Faulkner's subtle manipulation of sexual dynamics and gender roles within the novel illustrates the full complexity of his presentation of power and authority. The Father may exercise the linguistic power of naming, but the mother's foreign tongue complicates and undercuts the position of language within the Father's domain.

While the Father clearly exerts considerable figurative power, the Father's literal domain is curiously empty, for "real" fathers are largely absent in the book. In his careful analysis of the novel, François Pitavy examines the role of the father, noting the prevalence of father-figures (as opposed to fathers) which Joe acquires, and further establishes that "the grandfathers of Joe, Hightower, and Joanna could be seen as images and envoys of God the Father, the Almighty" (*Light* 45). But while these divine fathers encroach upon identity through their symbolic power, *Light in August*, like *Sanctuary*, attests to the power of the body. Mothers, with the exception of Lena, may come across as almost pathetically weak and victimized, but maternal power more than holds its own against divine paternity. Judith Bryant Wittenberg has observed that "the novel as a whole reveals in intriguing ways the problematic presence of the 'feminine' as an informing principle, the term 'feminine' denoting that which is dependent, emotional, and marginal—just as 'masculine' is that which is independent, rational, and culture-centered" ("Women" 104). While I question her definitions of masculine and feminine—Faulkner rarely categorizes things so neatly—I agree that the novel is shaped by what we might call a feminine principle and believe that an examination of this principle reveals Faulkner's anxieties about gender and language and the ways they interrelate.

Lena's childbearing, presented in a language unknown to men, indicates the presence of Irigaray's prediscursive reality which exposes the vulnerability of discursive reality. The mother precedes the naming power of God the Father, countering the power of the word. Thus the father's naming power, cited by Bleikasten, comes second. A child must be born before it can be named, the literal body must exist before it can be marked. When Byron hears Lena giving birth, he realizes that it *"was like me, and her, and all the other folks . . . were just a lot of words that never even stood for anything, were not even us, while all the time what was us was going on and going on without even missing the lack of words"* (402). Not only does Byron find himself, and the world, reduced to words, but they are words "that never even stood for anything, were not even us." The symbolic discourse of the father is revealed as a lack, while the essence behind the words— "what was us"—goes on without needing language, and is only uncovered at the moment of childbirth, that is, a moment of female creativity. Mothering, then, offers a counterforce to the linguistic control of the patriarchal tradition.

Paradoxically, Faulkner presents women's language as both foreign and intensely practical. Remembering Margaret Homans's assertion that women in literature are associated with literal discourse, while the more highly valued figurative discourse is conceived as masculine, we can see where Faulkner, like women writers, once again questions this split and the judgments it implies. If figurative creation is both masculine and linguistic, Lena's literal creativity must be presented in an anti-language. But hers is still a *language,* a discourse, for her creative maternal power is both literal and figurative. This novel, which may appear on the surface to present women as literal and men as figurative, also challenges and undercuts both this division and the valuation placed on the literal as opposed to the figurative. The literal, which often seems to trump figurative creation, questions the very premise of a book built on retellings and imaginative recreations.

If there is affirmation in the novel, it lies with Lena, the earth mother. Yet Byron is both attracted to and threatened by her literal creativity. His love for Lena allows him to recast her as an ideal woman, in other words, a virgin, despite the evidence of his own eyes. He meets Lena when she is nine months pregnant but cannot admit her pregnancy: "It was like for a week now his eyes had accepted her belly without his mind believing" (398–99). The eyes literally accept the condition of the woman, but the mind, instrument of figurative thought, cannot come to terms with what it means. By denying Lena's impending maternity, he hopes to erase the evidence not only of previous male possession but also of physical creativity. A man who spends his Saturdays working and his Sundays preaching, partly so he can stay out of trouble—away from women—Byron has clearly spent his life denying the sexual power of the body, sublimating it into work and religion. Finally confronted with what he has sought so strenuously to avoid, he finds himself utterly cut off, separated in both body and language from the maternal experience. Yet this separation does not impel him into the symbolic, for he never learns how to understand Lena's tongue. Indeed, Lena's maternal power essentially unmans Byron, as words, symbols of male power, lose their meaning.

But this unmanning, while it may explain why Byron functions as the least macho and sexist man in the text, does not help him to cross the gender gap. If even Byron—an almost feminized man—sees childbirth as part of an unknown language and finds himself forced to deny Lena's obvious sexuality, then the abyss between men and women is wide indeed. Underneath the pastoral comedy of Byron and Lena we find the same voids and disjunctions on which the more tragic sections of text are formulated; despite its multiple plot lines, *Light in August* is a tightly constructed novel in which men are constantly confronted with the power of the literal. In response, they continually attempt to re-impose figurative power by rewriting the women, and they generally succeed only in mis-creating images of the women they encounter.[1] By re-creating women as figures of male imagination, they hope to control feminine power, but the literal truth of femininity defies the reality which men would impose upon it. Lena breaks out of her male-constructed image, thus overturning figurative discursive dominance. Men may have figurative power; in this novel, however, as in much of Faulkner's work, that power is sadly misused, often creating a trap for those who wield it.

Consider, for example, Lena's opening scenes. Armstid, apprehensive about his wife's reaction, rather grudgingly takes her home, thinking, "*I know exactly what Martha is going to say*" (13), sure that she will repudiate the unwed mother. Armstid, however, is rather surprised to have Martha turn on him with the remark, "You men, . . . You durn men" (16). Martha responds to the situation by attacking not the sinning woman but a man, and even an innocent one at that. The division between them becomes more apparent when Armstid, contrary to his assumption, does not "know exactly" what Martha will do and has to ask her why she breaks the bank containing her egg money, the money which Lena will accept, "her face

pleased, warm, though not very much surprised" (23). The two women
seem to understand each other perfectly, Martha reading through Lena's
elaborate story, and Lena understanding Martha's brief, rather harsh responses. It is clear that they, at least, speak in the same tongue, while
Armstid remains outside their communion.

The ensuing action confirms this reading. Armstid deposits Lena at
Varner's store, where the men watch her approach, each one sure he knows
exactly what is on her mind, "that she is thinking of a scoundrel who
deserted her in trouble and who they believe that she will never see again."
Faulkner, however, has a different tale to tell. "She is not thinking about
this at all. She is thinking about the coins knotted in the bundle beneath
her hands [Martha's egg money] . . . thinking how she can enter the store
this moment and buy cheese and crackers and even sardines if she likes"
(26). Not only do the men fail to understand her, but their reading would
place her in a male-centered world, thinking of the man who impregnated
her. Lena, however, is thinking in practical, literal terms about what she
has—money—rather than what she has not—a man. While Lucas Burch
may live in her body, he does not seem to take up too much space in her
mind.

This female emphasis on the literal both illustrates and complicates
Homans's argument about women writers and their perception of the split
between the literal and figurative. The men would place Lena in a realm if
not figurative, at least more imaginative, in that they assume she is thinking about something other than her immediate present. The women,
however, tend to stick to the practical. In this Faulkner illustrates the
cultural dictum that figurative discourse is a male prerogative. Yet not all
of Lena's thoughts focus on literal reality. She is also, more than any other
character in the novel, a creator of fictions. When she leaves her brother's
house, she climbs out the window during the night, though she "could
have departed by the door, by daylight. Nobody would have stopped her.
Perhaps she knew that" (6). She travels under the name of Mrs. Burch and
imagines that upon her arrival Lucas "will see me and he will be excited"
(9).

Most importantly, she creates the fiction of her quest itself, of seeking
out Lucas Burch despite all the skepticism she encounters regarding its
probable success. That she continues the quest after Lucas's second departure clearly indicates his refusal to acquiesce in her plans suggests that
finding him was never her chief concern; traveling was, as I will discuss

later. Even more than Joanna's desperate belief in a non-existent pregnancy, more than Byron's willful blindness to Lena's condition, and more than Gail Hightower's constant replaying of the same stories told him years ago, Lena's imaginative fantasies celebrate fictionality itself and the process of figurative creation. Unlike other fictions in the novel, Lena's harmless stories fool and injure no one, including herself. They do indicate, however, that she has the figurative capability to live outside of her body as well the procreative ability within that body. By recasting her world as more interesting, more romantic, she integrates the figurative and literal, providing herself with a world in which her physical condition warrants no concern, for the Lord will see that a family will "all be together when a chap comes" (21). Her imaginative success can be measured by the degree to which she is able to make these fictions come true, to literalize them.

The men in the novel, however, who lack her grounding in the literal, cannot match her figurative success. One of the main problems in this book (and in most of Faulkner's work) is that men cannot understand women; often, this is because the men are too busy theorizing to see practical reality. Gail Hightower's inability to live outside of his imaginative fantasies causes his wife to kill herself, an action he cannot begin to understand until after delivering Lena's child, because he cannot perceive life except in figurative terms. In fact, he cannot even "see her [his wife] at all because of the face which he had already created in his mind" (479). The male-engendered figurative has obliterated the actual, with devastating effects for both. Only participation in events of the body such as Lena's childbearing, Joe's murder and castration, and his own physical injury, can awaken Hightower from his imaginative fantasies. The realization that he is "the instrument of her despair and death" because he has "not even been clay" but "a single instant of darkness in which a horse galloped and a gun crashed" (491), forces Hightower to recognize the importance of "being clay," of the physical. Yet his realization comes too late, for at Hightower's final moment in the novel (whether or not it is the final moment of his life) he again hears "the wild bugles and the clashing sabres and the dying thunder of hooves" (493).

From the very start of this novel we see the failure of male imagination to understand the female psyche. In some ways this failure makes Lena one of the most threatening figures in the text. The literal truth of Lena's thoughts and actions destroys the myths which the men create about her. Her denial of male-established order threatens the patriarchal community far more than Joe Christmas's violence. Joe's influence can, to some extent, be exorcised; Lena, however, passes out of the text in the wake of yet another male-engendered "explanation" of her motives and character. Because she remains "literal," she paradoxically remains distanced and mysterious. As long as the literal and figurative are dissociated, the gap between men and women cannot be healed.

Lena, moreover, is not the only woman to contend with, though she is often isolated in discussions of women in the novel. Varied as the women of *Light in August* are, they all share one very important attribute: the ability to disrupt and overturn patriarchal standards of order. From Lena, whose placidity in the face of desertion undercuts the standard patriarchal family with a man at its head, to Mrs. McEachern, who attempts to undo her husband's rigid Calvinist discipline, to Mrs. Hines, who tries to circumvent both her husband and the law in saving her grandson, to Joanna Burden, such a "masculine" woman that it seems to Joe "like I was the woman and she was the man" (235), women undercut masculine power and authority. Joanna in particular, Joe Christmas's counterpart in more than name, holds a crucial position in Faulkner's world. Like Joe, Joanna breaks down seemingly unassailable boundaries; she seems to undercut gender differentiation, while he erases racial distinctions. Just as much an alien outcast as Joe, Joanna challenges the community security in different and almost more threatening terms than Joe, for the issues which she represents are far less clear cut, less black and white, so to speak. Whereas Joe's death scene symbolically purges his black blood, murdering Joanna does not expel the feminine.

Both a Yankee and second-generation southerner, Joanna is of the community yet ostracized, her history intimately connected with the town, yet unacknowledged by the community. Joanna is a masculine woman in a world which, as it demonstrates by the way Lena Grove is sheltered and aided, values traditional feminine roles. However, her perceived masculinity does not extend to sexuality, for her kinky sexual desires set her apart from the asexual, yet very pregnant, Lena. Maternity rather than sexuality seems to determine femininity. Thus she is damned on two fronts—for excessive sexuality and for lack of female identity. Indeed, her imagined pregnancy may reflect a desire to solidify her gender, much as she uses it to demand that Joe solidify his race. Yet Joanna does not exist solely as sexuality embodied any more than Lena exists as maternity embodied. In addition to eagerly engaging in sexual intercourse, she and

Joe talk, discussing everything from family identity to race relations. Furthermore, her life has been determined not by her sexual "phase," which functions as an aberration rather than a defining characteristic, but by her vision of African Americans "not as people, but as a thing, a shadow in which I lived, we lived, all white people, all other people. . . .And I seemed to see the black shadow in the shape of a cross" (253). This imaginative notion of the "black shadow" marks her as a woman who knows how to reconcile the literal and figurative, for she lives her life as a practical expiation for the sins of racism, supporting "a dozen negro schools and colleges through the south" (233). Regardless of whether this simply constitutes a form of the white woman's burden, Faulkner presents it as an integration of imagination and practicality, creating a woman who operates in both realms.

Joanna is most often aligned with Joe Christmas in critical analysis, but Joanna and Lena, the two principal women, provide an equally interesting and less discussed comparison.[2] Standing at opposite ends of a spectrum of female sexuality, one a nymphomaniac going through menopause and the other a serene, almost asexual earth mother, these two figures confront each other across as wide a gulf as that separating any of the other pairs in the novel. Lena's maternity, less powerful and threatening to the community, on account of her class and marital status, than maternity generally is in Faulkner's work, seems natural; young rural women should be barefoot and pregnant, as Lena is for much of the novel. Joanna, on the other hand, whose sexuality and racial beliefs alienate her from the community, appears as unnatural. Joe is the thread that ties Lena and Joanna together, and since his connection to Lena is tenuous at best, the relationship between Joanna and Lena is weaker still. Lena enters town the day after Joanna's murder, and gives birth to her baby in the shack on Joanna's land. Lena is easily accommodated into the community, her "sin" readily tolerated, if not forgiven, by all she meets. Joanna, on the other hand, a lifelong resident, is followed on the streets by the call "Nigger lover!" (292). In short, the women are so different in all but gender that we must struggle to find a common ground on which to discuss them. Yet their gender aligns them; to ignore the connection tends to isolate Lena as an earth goddess, a life-giving force, which her association with Joanna undercuts.

In addition to their ability to disrupt patriarchy, one interesting similarity in their careers is that, both strong women, they nonetheless become passive recipients of southern chivalry. Lena seems to elicit protective

responses from most of the men she meets, from Armstid to Byron Bunch
to the furniture salesman at the end. Never asking for aid, she still generates both practical help in the form of food, shelter, and money and also
protective silence: Armstid does not tell her that the Burch at the planing
mill is really named Bunch, and Byron withholds crucial information about
Burch's whereabouts and activities. While the food and shelter certainly
help her along, the more subtle, and figurative, form of protection—
keeping the truth from a delicate female—turns out to be pointless. When
informed that Burch is really Bunch, she proceeds without concern—and
ultimately is proved right, when it turns out that the elusive Burch also
resides there. Later, Byron realizes that he has been uselessly keeping from
her what she already knows—that Burch is worthless and faithless. "I
never even had any need to keep it from her, to lie it smooth. It was like
she knew beforehand what I would say, that I was going to lie to her" (301–
02). Not only does Lena read through Lucas Burch, she also reads through
Byron Bunch, rendering his protective services and delicacy comically
inappropriate. She needs no figurative fantasies woven around her by
others.

Clearly, this chivalry benefits the men who offer it more than it benefits
Lena herself. Until confronted with Lena's unknown tongue during childbirth, Byron lives in the illusion that he is necessary to her, that he is,
therefore, important. But childbirth, the exclusively female ritual, explodes
such delusions of male dominance and forces Byron to recognize not just
her lack of virginity but the reality of literal creation. He has been imagining a figurative damsel in distress and is ultimately confronted with the
practical result of a sexually active woman. He thus becomes merely an
accessory to the mysterious and creative process of childbirth. Although
chivalry cannot accommodate such complex situations, as Byron finally
realizes, he continues to squire her across the state for his own sake, as he
now recognizes. For Lena needs no protection, not even against him, as
the furniture salesman remarks of Byron's futile and feeble attempt at
seduction/rape, "I be dog if I dont believe she picked him up and set him
back outside on the ground like she would that baby" (503). Ultimately
then, Lena manages to subvert and reverse chivalry, as she herself determines Byron's final destiny: "Aint nobody never said for you to quit" (506).
Unlike the pregnant woman of Wild Palms with whom she is often paired,
Lena controls the journey.

Joanna, on the other hand, inspires southern chivalric lynch law by her death. White women, no matter how unpopular while alive, must be avenged and posthumously protected. The move to unearth her murderer marks the first acknowledgment by the community of her presence within it. By forcing her into the position of the violated woman, creating a figurative fantasy rather than confronting the literal woman, the town can erase the disturbing elements which her presence has inspired. In fact, the townspeople revel in the situation; being murdered is the best thing she ever did for them, and they "hoped that she had been ravished too: at least once before her throat was cut and at least once afterward" (288). Not until Brown "reveals" Christmas's blackness does chivalry begin to take effect, however, as the community realizes it can now triumph over her, for her death erases the good works she has performed for the local African Americans and instead confirms the white community's racist view of the world. By essentially replacing Joanna with a stereotypic wronged white woman, the community exorcises the source of Joanna's power, which lay in her lack of conformity to such models. With the actual woman now dead, not there to refute directly the transformation, the male-dominated communal voice can redefine Joanna as a figurative emblem of the communal vision. In both cases, chivalry operates, not surprisingly, as an attempt to re-establish patriarchal order. Yet Faulkner demonstrates its failure to do so, as Lena shows herself perfectly capable of taking care of herself and we remember Joanna as she was in life, not as the community rewrites her after death.

What else can be gained from considering these two women together? One of the most crucial questions involves why Faulkner would have separated sexuality from procreation. Joe crushes Joanna's pathetic belief in her pregnancy with the brutal statement, "You just got old and it happened to you and now you are not any good anymore" (277). With the failure of this hope, Joanna is relegated to the sphere of the barren woman, as Hightower reflects, "Poor barren woman. To have not lived only a week longer, until luck returned to this place" (406). The "luck" he refers to, of course, is the birth of Lena's child. Certainly this birth does constitute one of the few positive emblems in the book. Why, then, must Joanna be so deliberately dissociated from it? Even though Pitavy identifies Joanna's house as a "womb image" (*Light* 99), there are no babies being produced here. It could be that her masculine role unfits her for the traditional female sphere. Her creativity, like masculine creativity, is restricted to the figurative realm as she indulges in sexual fantasies, with a particular "avidity for the forbidden wordsymbols" (258), and thus is left an "unfulfilled woman," neither wife nor mother.

It seems that Faulkner has made Joanna potentially too strong: her "masculine" character, sexual appetite, and vivid imagination coupled with literal procreative power would create almost a superwoman, a figure which Faulkner never fully actualizes. Every time he comes close—Joanna, Charlotte Rittenmeyer, Eula Snopes—he kills off the possibility by killing off or expelling the woman. Joanna is thus divided and sacrificed as a sexually repressed spinster, unable to become a real woman. The recollection of her strength, however, serves as a disturbing reminder of the potential power of women, power which it takes both death and a consequent figurative reformulation of her identity to eradicate. Furthermore, enough of Joanna remains in the literal characters of Joe and Lena to undermine her absence. Even the narrative structure rebirths her, for her story is told after her death is narrated, privileging the woman over the corpse.

Lena, on the other hand, remains as more than a memory, seemingly triumphant, though the question of how much real power she retains remains unresolved. Few people ever really triumph in Faulkner's work, and when we last see Lena, she is allegedly pursuing the same futile quest as when she entered. It could be that she and Byron will marry and settle down, but Faulkner clearly had no wish to confirm that reading. Lena moves off into the distance with yet another man interpreting her character. This last interpretation seems plausible and is not directly contradicted by the narrator, but that does not alter the fact that men are still speaking for her. Finally, the furniture salesman's words suggest a future which will undermine Lena's strength and any lasting victory:

> I reckon this was the first time she had ever been further away from home than she could walk back before sundown in her life. And that she had got along all right this far, with folks taking good care of her. And so I think she had just made up her mind to travel a little further and see as much as she could, since I reckon she knew that when she settled down this time, it would likely be for the rest of her life. (506)

Here again, we see a man deciding that all Lena ultimately wants is to settle down. If the salesman is correct, Lena's future is far from idyllic, which she fully recognizes. This venture represents her one excitement in life, the one time when she controls her direction. Once she marries Byron she will fulfill her role as wife and mother, and stay put for the rest of her life. So Lena's triumph appears at best qualified and at worst nonexistent; she is merely postponing the inevitable. The earth-mother role into which she has been cast does not offer any escape from a humdrum life; in fact, the two are closely related. Yet much as it purports to uphold it, Lena's position does undercut traditional stability. The essential gap between male and female comprehension has yet to be bridged, and it appears likely that it never will be. Settling down to marry Byron will not make Lena's motives and meanings any more apparent to men, for she exits the book on essentially the same terms as she entered it.

The conclusion of the novel attempts to divert our attention from the disruptive chaos of the text, for Lena's framing is read by most scholars as an affirmation, just as Lena herself is largely regarded as a life force. Sally Page claims that "through Lena Grove there is to be found both the fulfillment of life and the survival of humanity" (151), while Eric Sundquist finds that she "contain[s] the violence of the novel" (77). Given that much of the violence results from male reactions to incomprehensible women, she "contains" the violence much more literally (being a woman) than I think Sundquist implies. Yet the ending seems to be so patently a tacked-on "happy ending" that, considering the nature of what novel it concludes, it needs close scrutiny. Although it completes the opening frame, it seems foreign to much of the text. Rachel DuPlessis identifies "writing beyond the ending" as a narrative strategy of women writers, meaning "strategies that express critical dissent from dominant narrative" and "take issue with the mainstays of the social and ideological organization of gender" (5). Women writers and their textual surrogates find themselves marginalized by the conventional marriage plot, which imposes a strict closure on the female quest. Once again, it seems to me that Faulkner displays an awareness, generally attributed to women writers, of such marginalization and that he attempts to write beyond it.

Certainly Lena appears marginalized despite the fact that her words close the novel, for they are spoken not by her but by a man re-creating her as a story for his wife. Even if she herself is unaware of the marginalization, Faulkner must be, for he created it by creating the furniture salesman to speak for her. This subtle exaggeration of Lena's non-voice calls attention to itself even as it purports to silence her, creating a vague but definite uneasiness with the imposed closure. Yet even Lena's reconstructed words deny a marriage resolution, being concerned with her travels, her quest, rather than her potential husband. Thus the terms of the ending deny the closure which it appears to enforce. Furthermore, the ending leaves Joe Christmas far behind and thus seems to erase much of the text. Myra Jehlen writes that Lena's victory means little, for she "in no way speaks to the issues embodied in Christmas" (93). I agree that her victory means little; I even question its status as a victory, and in that questioning lies the relation to Joe, for the ambiguities which Lena embodies are mirrored in him. Race and gender are closely intertwined in this novel; closing with a woman does more to highlight than to deny the racial conflicts. As Carolyn Porter points out, Lena's famous line, "My, my. A body does get around" (507), gains "tragic profundity" when applied to "the body which gets around under the name of Joe Christmas" (Porter 255). The site of racial and sexual difference, the body ties the novel together.

The gender gap within the text in many ways is matched by the racial gap. The "Negro" and the "Female," as Maxwell Geismar forcefully puts it, are "the twin furies of Faulkner's deep southern Waste Land" (164). A close look at the career of Joe helps to illuminate the relationship between race and gender, the double crux of the novel. Joe encounters language barriers at an alarming rate, as he hears the "voices of invisible negroes" which "seemed to enclose him like bodiless voices murmuring talking laughing in a language not his" (114). Watching Joe Brown talk to Joe Christmas, Byron sees another instance of two people speaking different languages, "as if" Christmas "were a mile away, or spoke a different language from the one he knew" (40). Earlier in his career, when Joe first stumbles into the prostitution business which Max runs with Bobbie, he cannot quite understand what is going on; "it was as though they were speaking of him and in his presence and in a tongue which they knew that he did not know" (194). Clearly, Faulkner is carefully setting up this motif of a foreign language for a purpose. It is one of the connecting threads which weaves the halves of the novel together.

Yet as a thematic connection, this language gap functions in a somewhat paradoxical manner. For the communication gap is one of the main emblems of the disjunctive form of the novel. Thus it is itself both bridge and void. The fact of its being a motif common to both story lines certainly helps unify the book thematically, but the nature of the connection opens up more holes within the text. Through the figure of an unknown language, Faulkner illustrates not only the communication barriers between men and women and between blacks (or possible blacks) and whites, he also indicates that expression, language itself, is part of the problem. That we cannot even phrase the issue undercuts the connection, yet the common motif still suggests a link between race and gender, paradoxically united by this image of disjunction. The "bodiless voices" of the invisible negroes highlight the disjunction, for race is inscribed on the body. If the negroes are bodiless, can they be defined as negroes? With this image, Faulkner reminds us of the difficulties of determining literal racial difference; as a white man in Mottstown remarks, Joe "dont look any more like a nigger than I do" (349). The connection between bodies and race can be recast as that between literal and figurative, as racial difference, constructed figuratively in this novel, becomes just another fiction controlled, largely, by men.

This figurative difference, however, is literally imposed on Joe by a woman. He learns to associate race and gender early, thanks to the lessons of the dietitian. Crouching in the "rife, pinkwomansmelling obscurity behind the curtain" (122), Joe vomits up the sweet pink toothpaste which he associates with the "pink-and-white" dietitian, who thus discovers his presence in her room. Her face "no longer smooth pink-and-white, surrounded now by wild and dishevelled hair whose smooth bands once made him think of candy," she turns on him, screaming, "You little nigger bastard!" Vomiting, femininity, and blackness are intertwined for Joe, who thus associates race and gender not just with each other but with physical revulsion. Kristeva identifies vomiting as an expelling of the self, since food is not an "other." "I expel *myself, I spit myself* out, I abject *myself* within the same motion through which 'I' claim to establish *myself*. . . .I give birth to myself amid the violence of sobs, of vomit" (*Horror* 3). Born out of revulsion against blackness and femininity, Joe expels himself, and spends the rest of the novel seeking to recover that self.

Amid this violent physical "birth" we also see the origins of a textual birth, written on his "parchmentcolored" skin. "He was watching the pink worm coil smooth and cool and slow onto his parchmentcolored finger" (120). So often in literature, women's bodies are referred to as blank texts, "authored" by men. Here we see Joe as parchment, not only taking on that female role of the text for others write on, but being written on by femininity, the "pink worm." James Snead has asserted that "Joe is the uncertainty that resists being made into writing" (90). However, this scene inscribes the mark of femininity onto a body already possibly inscribed—in its parchment color—by race. Thus incription, textuality, takes the body as its vehicle, again integrating literal and figurative discourse.

Joe re-enacts this birth when confronted with the black girl in the shed years later, and he once again feels the urge to vomit: "There was something in him trying to get out, like when he had used to think of toothpaste" (156). He lashes out against the "womanshenegro," with a violence which can be explained by Kristeva's identification of vomiting with expulsion and birth. Lee Jenkins remarks that the girl "reminds him of the threat of nonbeing, as it reflects his blackness, and as it reflects the threat all women can present to the masculine ego in the form of absorbing and incorporating it back into what the men perceive as the abyss of the female self" (82). Yet Joe is not just confronting the abyss of the female self, for that female self is also his self. Joe, who constantly turns away from women, even seeking horses "because they are not women. Even a mare horse is a kind of man" (109), and who flaunts his lack of racial definition as his only means of identity, continually perceives race and gender as uniting in the ultimate threat to his being precisely because they are his being.

When he finds himself in "Freedman Town" he notices that the voices of "invisible negroes" surround him "talking laughing in a language not his" (114). Clearly Joe faces the same language gap as Byron, a situation which cannot be bridged with words because language creates the abyss. The reference to unknown language links the gender gap with the racial gap, but Faulkner goes on to make the connection much more explicit. Walking through the black section of town, Joe hears, "on all sides, even within him, the bodiless fecundmellow voices of negro women. . . .It was as though he and all other manshaped life about him had been returned to the lightless hot wet primogenitive Female" (115). The threat has become so pervasive that it has invaded his very being—"even within him," representing the "primogenitive," prediscursive reality of the mother.[3] The "abyss of the female self" threatens to take one "back" to a prediscursive stage uncontrolled by male language. Yet blackness, identified with femininity and revulsion, seems an integral part of the the threat, for these are black women's voices. Likewise, the "womanshenegro" incorporates his two sources of identity, the two forces which forced Joe's birth into abjection. However, the "womanshenegro" is transformed into "the She" several lines later, suggesting that for Joe, the feminine is ultimately more terrifying. Light in August is, after all, Faulkner's statement about the impossibility of using race as a biological determinant of behavior. He deliberately leaves Joe's racial identity unknown, to deny the reader the possibility of reading race as anything more than a sociological factor in identity, in contrast to gender, which cannot, of course, be literally erased.

This is not because the community doesn't try, however. Joe is castrated just before his death so that he will "let white women alone, even in hell" (464). As the townsmen watch him die with the "black blood" rushing out of him, "the *man* seemed to rise soaring into their memories forever and ever" (465, my emphasis). Joe's transcendence appears to rest on the obliteration of the literal, of race, as he becomes simply a man, but a man defined by a communal figurative vision. Yet the question remains as to whether Joe's "black blood" has literally been purged, whether it confirms or denies his racial status. As Snead puts it, "Whether 'black' is here a figurative or literal term is crucial but impossible to determine" (97). It makes sense that in a novel which moves between literal and figurative creativity, race, which depends on the distinction for its definition, should be left hanging between them. In fact, gender is left hanging as well, depending on whether the castration literally or figuratively obliterates his manhood. Noel Polk identifies Joe's last flight from the police as "a desperate ultimate repudiation of the mother, one last attempt to get the punishment he deserves" (91). But if he repudiates the mother by his flight, he also seems to end up re-engulfed in her, losing the masculine mark of difference from her. Even the language, as Pitavy notes, recalls that associated with femininity, with the serene Lena, for Joe's face is described as being "of itself alone serene" (Pitavy, *Light* 104, 105). In essence, Joe purges both race and gender in his transcendent death.

But we cannot forget that only linguistically can race and gender be eradicated, for bodies can be killed but not literally transformed. Joe may experience a figurative transcendence, but it does him no literal good whatever. He suffers literally from the sexual violence which the community has only wished on Joanna. Caught between the figurative and literal, masculine and feminine, black and white, Joe passes into the communal memory, an emblem of the impossibility of negotiating the multiple boundaries and discourses in the novel. There is no "catharsis," as Geismar says, in *Light in August* (167). The tension of the threat of race and gender, expressed both literally and figuratively, forms and shapes the novel, posing irreconcilable oppositions which Faulkner is too wise to attempt to bridge.

In fact, the form of *Light in August* with its double plot lines and lack of closure mirrors the uneasy relationships between the sexes and between the races. Sundquist notes that "the intersection of the three crises—of form, of blood, of history—lies in the embracing crisis of sexuality" (76). What women represent—silence, gaps, barriers—also functions as the structural framework of the novel. Donald Kartiganer calls the book "a tragic dialogue, a modern form in which design emerges as the voice of a chaos that is signified by and subverts that design" (39). If I substitute "woman" for "chaos," the statement, I think, still holds true. The design of the novel can be traced by the way that women are constructed, then deconstructed, attesting to creative power yet also subverting it in a dialogue between male voice and unknown female tongues. "In 'woman,'" says Julia Kristeva, "I see something that cannot be represented, something that is not said, something above and beyond nomenclatures and ideologies. There are certain 'men' who are familiar with this phenomenon; it is what modern texts never stop signifying: testing the limits of language and sociality" (*Feminisms* 137–38). Faulkner is one such man who, in "testing the limits of language," tests and challenges conventional conceptions of race and gender.

Faulkner said he began *Light in August* "with Lena Grove, the idea of the young girl with nothing, pregnant, determined to find her sweetheart" (*Univ.* 74). Regarding *The Wild Palms,* written, it is suggested, to stave off the heartbreak of his break-up with Meta Carpenter, the story he said he "wanted to tell" was of "the intern and the woman who gave up her family and husband to run off with him" (*Lion* 132), the young man who perfomed an abortion on his lover and, in so doing, killed her. In both cases, while Faulkner's initial vision comprised only a piece of what would emerge, both kernels elicit love stories: Lena Grove's tale of desertion by Lucas Burch, which leads to her probable union with Byron Bunch, and Harry Winterbourne's star-crossed affair with Charlotte Rittenmeyer, culminating in her death and his imprisonment. Clearly, love takes very different directions in these two novels, and pregnancy in *Light in August* leads to birth, not death. Amid these differences, however, these two books bear considerable similarity in their multi-plot structures, their pairing of a procreating and a murdered woman, and their evocation of the language gap as central to the problems between men and women. While Faulkner develops this last theme more fully in *Light in August, Wild*

Palms also examines the role of language, not just in human relations but in artistic creativity.

Too close a comparison to *Light in August* may gloss over some significant differences. Both novels set up a dichotomy between a fertile, pregnant woman and a masculinized woman. But just as the gulf between Lena and Joanna may be less vast than initially supposed, the distance between Charlotte and the unnamed pregnant woman is narrower still. Most obviously, both are mothers. Charlotte, while sharing some of Joanna's masculine qualities as well as some of her sexual appetite, has given birth twice and is poised to do so again. While *Wild Palms* offers a more explicit portrayal of maternity than *Light in August,* its impact is felt more in the ways that the men are shaped by maternal power than in the women who embody it.

The difference between the two women of *Wild Palms* is not their birthing ability; it is their relation to figurative and literal creativity. Much more than Lena, the pregnant woman seems to function as a walking womb. She rarely speaks and apparently acquiesces to all of the convict's heroic efforts to rid himself of her. But despite her status as object, she comprises a curious combination of the literal and figurative, existing both as a physical body and "all pregnant and female life" (153). Charlotte, on the other hand, is an artist, generally conceived as a figurative (and masculine) role, yet she creates both literal art objects and literal babies. With an equal command of language and a much stronger command of procreation than Joanna Burden, she explicitly questions the divisions and connections between art and maternity. In her, Faulkner opens up the possibility of a woman who combines sexuality, maternity, and linguistic power, only to close it off when she rejects her maternal capability by insisting on an abortion.

Even critics sympathetic to Charlotte tend to identify procreation as artistically positive and to conclude, as Laurie A. Bernhardt does, that her "most important flaw—her inability to see love, like art, as a creative, life-giving act—leads to her tragedy" (364). Janet Carey Eldred argues, "But finally we are to realize that this female creative power, this 'dominating feminine impulse' is a threat to the race" (156). Clearly women's creativity is a crucial issue in this novel, yet one which depends on context, on the story and on the men she encounters. While the plot does squelch the mother, killing one and turning the other over to a deputy, the novel moves back and forth—almost in the point-counterpoint pattern Faulkner identified as the structural relation between the two narrative lines—between literal and figurative power, maternal and artistic creativity. Regardless of what happens to literal mothers, maternal creative power exercises considerable sway.

Charlotte, who glories in the fact that she and Harry are constantly recognized for what they are, or rather, what they are not—"we just dont look married, thank God" (108)—may not look married, at least, not married to Harry, according to the real estate agent who "can smell a husband" (8). She does, however, look like a mother, as the doctor immediately senses. *"She has borne children,* he thought. *One, anyway; I would stake my degree on that"* (11). Charlotte seems to exude an air of maternity, possibly the smell that Harry lacks. This emanation of motherhood suggests that maternal status can be perceived, that is, perceived by those trained in medicine, those with an intimate scientific knowledge of women's bodies. In fact, Faulkner goes to some lengths to establish that this doctor's knowledge is medical rather than sexual by implying that his marriage is sterile and possibly chaste.

> On the evening of the wedding he and his wife went to New Orleans and spent two days in a hotel room, though they never had a honeymoon. And though they had slept in the same bed for twenty-three years now they still had no children. (4)

By including this revelation of the doctor's sexless marriage, Faulkner offers a reason for his limited understanding of the complicated human relationships in front of him, and thus implicitly privileges experience over science, sexuality over mind. In thus reversing the expected hierarchy of mind over matter, Faulkner reduces the doctor to an asexual body, a quivering mass of self-righteous and frightened anger against women who reject maternity and men who act as both lover and abortionist. While his medical degree renders him able to diagnose maternity, thereby suggesting that it can be viewed as some kind of disease, he is singularly inept at determining anything else about Charlotte. Abortion complications seem a new arena for him. He may be able to stake his degree on the fact of Charlotte's maternity, but not on her choice to avert it. Science can only diagnose—and accept—what is culturally expected of women: motherhood. Thus despite the fact that he senses that she may be listening to "the secret irreparable seeping of blood" (5), he draws back from what would be a surprisingly accurate diagnosis, and concludes that the lungs must be at fault. His more philosophical explanation is that her problem is hatred, *"Not at the race of mankind but at the race of man, the masculine"* (11). But his theory fails to convince, for such hatred is difficult, if not impossible, to trace in Charlotte, who goes out of her way to placate Rat and to protect Harry. Even while delirious, a time when "truth" might emerge, she reiterates her exoneration of "that bastard Wilbourne" (21) to the extent of claiming to be a whore in order to shield him.

Thus the doctor's conclusions reveal more about him than her. His readiness to connect a woman's adultery with hatred of the masculine indicates his own sense of uneasiness regarding women, further confirmed by his resentment at being forced to acknowledge the full situation before him. Both too young and too old to be able to say, *"Thank God I am not him"* (17), the doctor feels uncomfortably implicated in the sexuality he has avoided all his life. He evidently feels some jealousy towards Harry, but his assumption of Charlotte's hatred must shield him from some of his sexual disappointment. The doctor, who feels that he "had been both fortunate and right in having been elected to lose" passion, finds himself at a loss in the face of it (279). He now must deal not simply with passion but with the literal results of destructive male sexuality—a dying female body; Harry has both impregnated Charlotte and aborted the fetus, has penetrated her with both his body and his knife. The impotent doctor, with his "thick soft woman's hands" (4), can neither duplicate Harry's feat nor restore his victim to life. Rendered as helpless as Harry, he goes to ridiculous lengths to distance himself from him.

His ludicrously excessive behavior—waving around a pistol and making wild threats against a man who clearly has no interest in escaping—is an attempt to assert masculine control over a situation which reminds him of his own lack of masculinity. The gun, "a cheap-looking nickel-plated revolver such as you could find in almost any pawnshop and which, as far as serviceability was concerned, should still have been there" (289), is a wholly inadequate phallic symbol which further reflects the doctor's emasculation. The man of healing turns out to be not much of a healer and not much of a man, just as Harry proves himself not much of an abortionist. When faced with pregnancy and its repercussions, both lose skill and even gender.

If maternity itself can be threatening to male autonomy, the choice to terminate a pregnancy uncovers male impotence and the fragility of masculine identity. This opening chapter, with its beleaguered men trying desperately to retain their masculine identities in the face of Charlotte's de-maternalized body, sets the tone for a novel in which the fixity of women's biological difference paradoxically challenges the boundaries of gender. Just as maternal power can be expressed both literally and figuratively, thus debunking the Lacanian identification of discursive reality as falling under the Law of the Father, so gender identity overruns its expected boundaries, calling into question the most basic ways we categorize people: as men and women. Faulkner consistently questions cultural definitions of gender, and this novel, in particular, reveals their tenuous nature. Numerous critics have identified Charlotte as masculine. In general, however, it is masculinity rather than femininity which is in short supply in the book.

Despite Harry's recognition that Charlotte stares at him "like a man might" (39), that she is both a "better man" (133) and a "better gentleman" (141) than he is, she comes across as profoundly feminine. She becomes, for Harry, representative of all women, as he constantly watches her and muses on the predilections women have for cohabitation, liaisons, and renting bathrooms. She arranges her hat with what he identifies as "the immemorial female gesture out of the immemorial female weariness" (124). Regardless of the attention paid to her alleged masculine attributes, Charlotte lives as a woman and dies a woman's death. Gendering her as masculine suggests a reluctance to classify as feminine a woman who speaks her desires clearly and asserts her will forcefully. It is less threatening to speak of masculine women than to admit that masculinity itself may be a flawed concept.

In Harry's case, masculinity is not just a flawed concept but an absent one. He compares himself to a "middleaged eunuch" (34) and writes pulp fiction under a woman's name. He takes a largely passive role in the relationship, though his few assertions of will are striking: he decides to keep the wallet and cash he finds to finance their initial journey to Chicago, and later he insists that they leave Chicago for Utah in the dead of winter. In the first instance, he essentially commits robbery, robbing not the mother but a garbage bin, which nets him not creativity but cash. Consequently, he neither writes a poem nor sculpts a grecian urn; rather, he ends up producing soft-core pornography and a dead woman. He seeks not to be an artist but to live an unrespectable life, a life which lacks the conventional woman's touch. Yet rather than escaping from the feminine sphere, he finds himself expelled from the realm of the Father. Beginning with a crime, he sets himself outside law and society and casts off the protection which law and culture might offer. Having cast himself adrift into what he later calls "the pervading immemorial blind receptive matrix, the hot fluid blind foundation—grave-womb or womb-grave" (138), he loses stability of self and, ultimately, individual autonomy as he returns to an embryonic state.

Harry's next assertion of will comes when he decides he has come too close to respectability, too close to comfort. He also appears to have come too close to a feminine identity through writing women's stories and being at least partially supported by Charlotte, and somehow decides that Utah may be less respectable—and thus more masculine—than Chicago. In his longest sustained conversation, he tries to explain to McCord the reasons behind his decision to seek out the wilderness in February, and he credits Charlotte with making a new man of him: "there is something in me that she is not mistress to but mother" (141). This is one of the few moments in Faulkner's work where a man appears to feel a gain from having been "mothered," though Harry stresses that this has been a completed birth, that rather than returning to the womb he has become a new man. However, his rebirth out of the "grave-womb or womb-grave" leads him not to autonomy but to a near engulfment in snow and ultimately to total engulfment in prison.

Harry presents the move to Utah as a moral stand, a rejection of the tame feminine life. He abjures social law for the laws of love and the wilderness. But however admirable the action itself may be, the dubious nature of the enterprise, an obviously crooked scheme whereby he need only pretend to be a doctor, undermines his moral stance against the corruption of financial security. The mine company needs not his skills—his professional masculine identity—but his bodily presence:

> I dont care two damns in hell how much or how little surgery and phar-
> macology you know or dont know or how many degrees you might have
> from where to show it. Nobody else out there will; there'll be no State
> inspectors out there to ask to see your license. I want to know if you can be
> depended on to protect the mine, the company. Against backfires. Suits
> from wop pick-and-shovel men and bohunk powder-monkeys and chink
> ore-trammers. (128)

In accepting this post Harry denies his mind and compromises his ethics. He becomes a kind of outlaw, a man who does not uphold masculine civilization and culture.

Furthermore, in trying to assert his masculine identity by going off into the wilderness like a modern-day Daniel Boone, he finds himself lacking in the expertise needed and so only flounders in snow drifts, as vulnerable to the environment as to Charlotte's dominance. Thus his assertion of masculinity, rather than entrenching him in the symbolic, returns him to the literal, while at the same time highlighting his physical limitations, his lack of independence in this literal world. Both of Harry's moments of action, then, are associated with a regression back to infancy, revealing the fragility of his masculine identity. To act like a man ungenders him, for it renders him vulnerable to becoming symbolically reintegrated with the mother, to losing autonomy and thus, as Lacan would have it, being denied participation in the realm of the Father.

Indeed, Harry experiences considerable difficulties with symbolic discourse. His greatest verbal endeavor—the attempt to explain himself to McCord—is so confused and convoluted as to be very difficult to follow. His words mean nothing to the Poles at the mine, while Charlotte's drawings explain the situation clearly. Even when he manages to articulate his needs, his language fails to achieve its aims. He has great difficulty persuading anyone to give him a job and gets thrown out of a brothel for demanding a referral to an abortionist. Most importantly, he fails to convince Charlotte to carry the fetus to term. If the ability to impose law and master language are identifying features of masculinity, Harry comes up short.

Neither does he succeed in the feminine world of Mother Nature. While living in the cabin on Lake Michigan, he gleefully believes that he has used "Nature the unmathematical, the overfecund . . . to prove his mathematical problem for him" (114) in drawing up a calendar based on Charlotte's menstrual cycles. He tries to employ the physical sign of women's procreative power in the service of mathematical calculations, hoping to subordinate bodies to science. Nature, however, gets the last word, for once he determines the exact date to be November 12, he feels betrayed by an "old whore" (115) who provided an Indian summer, thus lulling him into believing that winter was still distant. Given that they are living in the woods, presumably until the cold drives them out, exact dates mean nothing. The weather should rule their actions. But Harry cannot submit to Mother Nature. His outrage and his overtly gendered remarks about nature as "Lilith," a "bitch," and a "whore" reveal his hostility to femininity. He lacks the facility to operate in a feminine world as well as a masculine one, his failure reflecting the dangers of gendered identity. Neither a doer nor a speaker, Harry seems not so much feminized as emasculated. Yet he does have one obvious source of power, for he survives while Charlotte does not. Despite his cultural emasculation, he has a body which does not reproduce, and so does not require maintenance with a knife. Granted that he ends up in jail, deciding to take grief over nothing, he still has a choice denied Charlotte. Gender may be fluid, both dangerous and encroaching, but bodies still determine life and death.

Despite her tragic and wasteful death, Charlotte stands as one of Faulkner's strongest women. While there have been many negative critical responses to her, such as that by Thomas L. McHaney who accuses her first of "snaring the innocent Wilbourne into her scheme" (31) and then of destroying their life together by prostituting herself making money with her "perverted art" (74), more recently some positive readings have emerged. Bernhardt defends her courage and her belief in the importance of love, and Eldred re-examines her role as artist, linking it to the creative metaphors of the novel. Anne Goodwyn Jones writes that Faulkner treats Charlotte "with a respect . . . that is absent from his treatments of other sexually active and assertive and intelligent women: Joanna Burden's unbelievable sexual games come to mind" (145). Like Joanna Burden, though, Charlotte finds that sexuality leads inexorably towards death. Experiencing the pregnancy which Joanna apparently only fantasizes, Charlotte, asserting that children "hurt too much" (217), refuses to carry the fetus to term. Her literal rejection of mothering, unique in Faulkner's work, (though Dewey Dell Bundren actively seeks an abortion), reflects a desire for autonomy, for the opportunity to live her own life. Even willing to abandon the children she has already borne, Charlotte seeks creativity through art and love rather than childbirth.

Her endeavors in both are closely tied to the body. A woman with a keen sexual appetite, she insists that she and Harry consummate their relationship on the train in order to overcome the temptation to return to Rat. Once they have sealed their love with their bodies, she can find the strength to resist the pull of husband and children. Later, in Utah after her douche bag bursts, she continues to engage in sexual intercourse without informing Harry, who might refuse. She wants to believe "that when people loved, hard, really loved each other, they didn't have children, the seed got burned up in the love, the passion" (205). Her body, of course, betrays her belief in the incendiary power of passion; love, as an abstract concept, does not burn up the seed which its physical manifestation implants. Bernhardt, though largely sympathetic to Charlotte, criticizes her for her "ideal of love, [which] for all of its passion and its sacrifice, is essentially a sterile one, because it is an abstraction that can be only briefly embodied in the flesh of worthy lovers, and cannot, therefore, endure" (359). While it may seem paradoxical to describe Charlotte's view of love as both an abstraction and a physical embodiment, the one associated with a figurative mode and the other with the literal, such an opposition exactly describes Charlotte's attempted transcendence of gender. However, rather than decrying the paradox as sterile and unenduring, which seems to condemn her for rejecting maternity, I would point to Charlotte's attempts to negotiate between the literal and figurative and marvel that she succeeds as well as she does.

Charlotte is not a woman of many words, though she certainly has more than the pregnant woman of "Old Man." Nevertheless, when she does use language she articulates her ideas clearly. She persuades Harry to give Billie an abortion because they are in trouble and, most of all, because "this is for love too. Not ours maybe. But love" (194). Her own reason for wanting one, though Harry at first has difficulty understanding it, is also clear and concise: children hurt too much. Harry, who initially reads the hurt literally, uses the argument that despite the pain, women have borne children for ages. His inability to read beneath the literal meaning marks him as less linguistically adept than Charlotte; she knows—and says— exactly what she means. Her silence in the cottage on the coast, rarely broken except in delirium and excessive pain, suggests not that she can find no words but that words are of no more use. Her last sustained verbal effort is to persuade Rat to protect Harry. Having taken care of that, she seems to abjure the symbolic, focusing her attention instead on her own body. Her downfall has been from physical not linguistic causes: her own pregnancy and Harry's trembling hands, which botch the abortion. Charlotte knows both when to use language and when her condition is beyond it.

Even in art, a field defined largely by the symbolic, Charlotte attempts to literalize abstraction, to produce "something you can touch, pick up, something with weight in your hand . . . that displaces air and displaces water" (41). As a sculptor she literalizes the figurative, but in so doing provides the metaphor for her own defeat. Eldred's excellent article argues that the central metaphor of the novel is that of the still life, of Charlotte's stated desire to capture motion in her art. "Indeed, both as an artist and a woman, Charlotte will still life through 'artificial' means. For in *The Wild Palms,* as in other novels, metaphors for creativity are extended into character and plot, are 'literalized'" (Eldred 149). However, as Eldred points out, Charlotte's desire to "still life" leads to her literal death. This literalization of the figurative does indeed follow the pattern Margaret Homans identifies, equating the process with a turning toward death, especially for women. A woman artist is still a woman with a woman's body.

Thus despite the novel's seemingly fluid gender boundaries, a fluidity which Minrose Gwin persuasively equates with the feminine, the boundaries between the sexes also remain rigidly drawn. *The Wild Palms* offers a curious mixture of fluidity and separation in its form and within both narratives. I would like to suggest that the collision between fluidity and solidity throughout the novel can be read as a struggle with maternal power. Barbara Johnson says of Mallarmé that the blank spaces in the text of his poems "do not simply make the mother present; they recreate the drama of the simultaneity of attachment and detachment that defines the maternal *function*" (141). This drama of attachment and detachment can be seen in the relationship between the two parts and amongst the characters themselves, who struggle between engulfment and autonomy, between fear and envy of a maternal function which represents home and not-home, the uncanny source of life and death.

"Old Man," which both attaches to and detaches from "Wild Palms," shares its uneasiness with gender boundaries and maternal power. John Feaster identifies the jail as "a perfect institutionalized mother-archetype" (90) to which the convict wishes desperately to return but is prevented by the Father, the Old Man. François Pitavy agrees, suggesting that the all-male prison (and the hospital where Harry initially works) are "safe, maternal places, where the sense of security and comfort are compounded by the expected duties and the reassuring routine" ("Forgetting" 122). Curiously, both define a "maternal place" by security rather than gender. While I would challenge "security and comfort" as characteristic attributes of maternal space, I agree with the identification itself with one significant qualification: these are maternal places without mothers and without women. A figurative maternal place without literal reminders of literal maternity offers the comfort of the mother without her disturbing power. Both Harry and the convict leave these havens to go out into a world where they are dominated by masculine figures: Charlotte and, particularly, the Old Man. "The 'Old Man' is really the one father figure in the novel, or rather the forefather, the creator of the American land" (Pitavy 121). Yet just as the maternal prison is populated with men, blurring its gender, so the Old Man can be read as both masculine and feminine. Gwin, drawing on earlier work of Gail Mortimer, claims that the flooding river represents femininity, a "multiple and mutual process of reproduction. As Faulkner himself well knew, a river—particularly the Mississippi River—reproduces itself by flooding, creating new flows" (Gwin 125).

Father or mother? The validity of both interpretations attests to the difficulty of gendering this novel which is, at the same time, so intensely gendered. Gender is only absolute when women are giving birth or dying from abortion complications. This solidification of gender in the female body—one does not "put on" pregnancy—renders the mother the only truly gendered figure. This stability may be precisely what causes the extreme discomfort the male characters feel for women, particularly for mothers. Once Harry realizes that Charlotte is pregnant he panics, spending his days wallowing in snow drifts and then making a ludicrous search for an abortion drug which he knows doesn't exist. The tall convict only wants to turn his back "on all pregnant and female life forever and return to that monastic existence of shotguns and shackles where he would be secure from it" (153).

Motherhood defines both women in the novel, granting them—or forcing them into—a sense of self which is intimately connected to the body. They display an ease with their bodies that is lacking in the men, as Charlotte walks around naked with an utter lack of self-consciousness and has no hesitation in submitting her body to Harry's knife. The pregnant woman, whose body must be fully displayed as she gives birth, never indicates any embarrassment over her condition. It is the convict who turns his eyes away, first from her stomach and then from the sight of her nursing her infant. The convict, however, seems more aware of, and in control of, his body than Harry. Harry "fumble[s] at the lock" of the drawing room on the train where he and Charlotte consummate their affair, and is unable to remove his clothes with his "clumsy fingers" (60), tragically foreshadowing Charlotte's death at his hands.

The tall convict, with his mock heroic bodily prowess, seems, in marked contrast to Harry, to be a manly man. He keeps his skiff afloat under nearly impossible conditions and paddles valiantly for days on end with little food or rest. He has a firm sense of purpose, even if born out of desperation, and, as Doreen Fowler has argued, upholds "order and responsibility"

("Measuring" 280). Unlike Harry, who seeks to establish himself outside of law and order, the convict longs for the familiar control of the state and keeps trying to surrender to the law.

Yet the tall convict also has his problems—with his body, with the law, with women, and with language. Despite his strength and determination in paddling, he fails to achieve his goals, in part because he cannot read the river. It is not just that the water defies nature and reverses its flow, but he rarely looks over the side of the boat. He twice strikes the same tree (with the woman sitting in it) without realizing it "because he had not yet looked higher than the bow of the boat" (146). Likewise, when the skiff passes Vicksburg, the "convict didn't know it. He wasn't looking high enough above the water" (157–58). Thus while he pushes his body to tremendous and almost inhuman exertion, his efforts are largely ineffectual because he fails to employ any techniques besides brute strength in his endeavors and neglects to focus on his physical surroundings. His body, without the help of greater mental understanding, delays his safe return.

The convict's body generally serves him well, but it does show signs of weakness. His nose bleeds frequently, causing him to believe that if the baby were to "shoot me in the tail with a bean blower my nose would bleed" (260). This periodic bleeding feminizes him by its suggestion of menstruation. In fact, Faulkner subtly highlights this implication with the comic interruption back at Parchman when the tall convict reports that the doctor aboard the steamship suggested that he might be hemophilic. The other convicts argue over whether this means "a calf that's a bull and a cow at the same time" or "a calf or a colt that aint neither one" (242). By evoking the word "hermaphrodite," the conversation links the tall convict to dual sexuality, to femininity. Indeed, his excessive anxiety to rid himself of his female passenger reflects an extreme discomfort with women, possibly a reaction to a latent femininity or homosexuality. The all-male haven he seeks certainly suggests the possibility of homoeroticism, particularly with the plump convict who wears "a long apron like a woman, [and] cooked and swept and dusted" (27). The tall convict's heroic physical masculinity, then, turns out slightly blurred along the edges.

Like Harry, the tall convict also has difficulties with language. The narrative is interspersed with comments about what he cannot or does not tell. When he is caught once again by the flooding river in the swamp, he finds the experience beyond words: "He could not have told this if he had tried" (269). Earlier, after he drags the skiff over an embankment, the narrator remarks, "he didn't tell how he got the skiff singlehanded up the revetment and across the crown and down the opposite sixty foot drop, he just said he went on" (251). In fact, the entire story which the convict is allegedly relating in Parchman, comes largely from the narrative voice, not the convict.

> He told it—of the next eight or nine days . . . while the four of them— himself and the woman and baby and the little wiry man . . . whose language neither of them could understand—lived in the room and a half. He did not tell it that way. . . .He just said, "After a while we come to a house and we stayed there eight or nine days then they blew up the levee with dynamite so we had to leave." That was all. (252)

The convict's inability to tell the details of his escapade is not particularly surprising; he is a man who has been betrayed by the power of storytelling by "accepting information on which they [writers] placed the stamp of verisimilitude and authenticity," and using such information to direct his attempted train robbery, which lands him in Parchman (23). Clearly, rhetoric is not his forte. Even before this epic adventure, which might challenge the rhetorical powers of someone more articulate than the convict, he finds himself at a loss for words. At his trial, outraged at the authors who misled him, he cannot express his feelings, leading to more fury. "So now [at Parchman] from time to time . . . he mused with that raging impotence, because there was something else he could not tell them at the trial, did not know how to tell them" (25). His inability to explain that he was after honor, not money, seems to cause him greater anger than his imprisonment. By associating this lack of verbal ability with impotence, Faulkner suggests that mastering symbolic discourse is connected to masculine power; to be silent—for a man—is to be impotent. Like Harry, then, the tall convict has not been fully integrated into the Law of the Father.

The convict, however, does manage to overcome the difficulty of different languages, a task Harry can accomplish only with Charlotte's visual aids. He communicates amazingly well with the Cajan, despite a language barrier so intense that it seems to the convict as if the Cajans speak "in a tongue he had never heard before" (244), which resembles animal sounds: "Gobble-gobble, whang, caw-caw-to-to" (240). The problem of speaking in different tongues recalls the difficulties in *Light in August* between Lena Grove and Byron Bunch and between Joe Christmas and the white world.

In "Old Man" the characters bridge this gulf partly by shared experience and partly by understanding. Even with the woman the convict communicates well, in contrast to the sometimes tortured, sometimes comic misunderstandings that prevail between Lena and Byron. The narrator suggests that she understands him "not from that rapport of the wedded conferred upon her by the two weeks during which they had jointly suffered . . . but because she too had stemmed at some point from the same dim hill-bred Abraham" (254–55). Understanding is not conveyed through words but through common background. Thus language becomes secondary to experience, a kind of prediscursive reality determined by the circumstances of one's birth. Once again, the mode of discourse associated with women succeeds where symbolic discourse fails.

Another language also succeeds: that of money. Because the two men have business interests in common, the convict does not need to speak. "Money aint got but one language" (255). They can create a pact "which both not only understood but which each knew the other would hold true and protect (perhaps for this reason) better than any written and witnessed contract" (260). This agreement made by mutual understanding, mutual interest, succeeds better than any legal document, perhaps because they understand it. Unlike a "written and witnessed contract," a shared understanding is not put down in legal jargon and thus liable to being misconstrued. Communication which does not depend on linguistic expression is more reliable than written and witnessed symbolic discourse. In fact, the two men speak not so much the language of money but the language of trading, of an economy which predates money. Just as the convict's understanding with the woman arises out of their common pasts, so his understanding with the Cajan relies on a practice associated with the past. Going back to origins—of birth and of culture—seems to be the key to bridging communication gaps.

Yet when the convict finds himself confronted with literal origin, he reacts with fear and loathing. Back at Parchman, in response to the plump convict's query as to why he got in trouble with another man's wife on the journey back up the river when he already had a woman at hand, the tall convict recalls "how there were times, seconds, at first when if it had not been for the baby he might have, might have tried. But they were just seconds because in the next instant his whole being would seem to flee the very idea in a kind of savage and horrified revulsion" (334–35). Even in the seconds when he considers the idea of having sex with the woman, he protects himself against the possibility by the reflection "if it had not been for the baby"; since the baby, of course, *is,* any consummation becomes impossible.

For the convict, in fact, sexual intercourse with this woman is not just impossible but unthinkable. The violence of his response to "the very idea" hints at a kind of incestuous attraction to the woman who represents an "inert monstrous sentient womb" (163). That womb, unlike the maternal prison, threatens his very being. At the infant's birth, Feaster points out, the convict experiences a kind of rebirth, slipping back into the water feet first in "a kind of psychodramatic reversal of the birth process" which suggests an "incomplete mastery of the initial birth separation" (Feaster 92). He then looks at the child and thinks,

> *This is what severed me violently from all I ever knew and did not wish to leave and cast me upon a medium I was born to fear, to fetch up at last in a place I never saw before and where I do not even know where I am.* (231)

The convict's identification with the baby helps to explain his revulsion against sex with the mother, but I find it curious that he seeks so desperately to return to what both Feaster and Pitavy have identified as a mother-substitute and womb image: the prison. Why flee from the mother to a surrogate mother?

The answer lies in the difference between symbolism and reality, figurative and literal. The convict prefers the figure, the substitute, to the thing itself. Womb imagery is safe only when it masquerades as an all-male enclave; seeing the literal womb in action inspires fear and revulsion. The prison offers the security of the mother without the body of the mother, in other words, the mother lacking creative power. This discomfort with women's bodies and procreative ability matches Byron Bunch's reluctance to admit Lena Grove's pregnancy. One idealizes—figures—women until their bodies get in the way. Charlotte, for example, can be an artist and romantic heroine only until her body takes over. The unnamed pregnant woman, whose body cannot be idealized away, is denied human status not only by the various references to her as "female meat" (170) but also by the convict's words to the deputy he finally surrenders to: "Yonder's your boat, and here's the woman" (278). He is returning the property entrusted to him.

Nevertheless, the power of the female body in this novel, as in so many of Faulkner's books, overcomes male attempts to control it. Charlotte certainly pays the price for attempting to isolate love from procreation because children "hurt too much." Much has been written on why she fails, how she fails, and whether she is to blame for failing. Her attempts to capture motion, to freeze the body, as Eldred points out, are literalized, as her own body stills its life. Yet the pregnant woman's role is often under-read by critics who look more closely at the "Wild Palms" section. She is, after all, the only major character left alive and free at the end of the book. She may be handed over to the deputy by the convict to be heard of no more, but the lack of closure to her story grants her a pervasive quality none of the other characters enjoy. Like Lena Grove, she seemingly wanders out of the novel, carrying with her the only life generated in the book and the only potential for continued procreation.

Even the tall convict's concluding words, "Women, shit!" (339), cannot touch her for she is gone while he is back subscribing to "rules" laid down not in the cause of justice but of political expediency. He may have the last words, but language has not served him well and thus becomes a poor substitute for creative power. He finally finds the words to tell his story in the last section of the book, but it has become a story of a return to safety, not an epic battle against the elements and the alligators.

> Then, suddenly and quietly, something—the inarticulateness, the innate and inherited reluctance for speech, dissolved and he found himself, listened to himself, telling it quietly, the words coming not fast but easily to the tongue as he required them. (332)

This may be read as the convict's final triumph in acquiring a voice. The words now come easily. Yet I think we must connect the words to the tale. He now tells a rather simple story of working his way back up the river. Thus I am less convinced that he has gained great powers of articulation than that he has now come to the part of the story which does not require great rhetorical facility. He can finally describe how he got rid of the woman. Distancing himself from the mother, he finds language as he moves into the realm of the Father.

However, if we accept the prison as a maternal space, the convict has not really separated himself at all. He has replaced the literal body of the mother with a figure and has mastered symbolic discourse as further evidence of his autonomy but has lost any artistic, heroic, or creative potential. The final gift of language comes only when it leads nowhere: "it was all done, finished, now and he was safe again, so maybe it wasn't even worth talking about any more" (331). Language is bred not out of safety but out of danger, out of the mother, precisely against whom it cannot be used. While talk may be an inadequate force against the power of the mother, it is also an inadequate replacement for her since it loses significance once separated from her. Symbolic discourse relates only tales of surrender, not of manly heroism.

There is, of course, a voice to relate the manly heroism: that of the unidentified narrator. It takes a disembodied voice to speak the body. The unnamed characters of "Old Man" lack the control over their tale that Harry exercises in "Wild Palms," where much of the narrative is filtered through his consciousness. His tale, however, is a tale of the death of a body and the imprisonment of a body. His decision to take grief over nothing ensures the continuity of his body but also privileges love as as figurative rather than physical experience, directly contrary to Charlotte's conviction. Women's lives—and women's voices—are indeed stilled, while the men return to the womb-prison, finding in language and grief a replacement, even though an inadequate one, for women. They have life but not autonomy, having been made (or remade) into components of a largely undistinguishable group, subject to being chained together with "clashing umbilicals" (67). Meanwhile, the womb remains, figured in the jail which now contains them, and embodied in the pregnant woman-turned-mother who now floats out of the book, uncontained and uncontainable. Maternity reveals its power to grant and deny life, but it still relegates women to their bodies. While this novel ultimately fails to sustain a mother-artist, it does, however briefly, embody the possibility.

Once again, the mother's body constitutes the center of the text, but these mothers, unlike those in Sound and the Fury and As I Lay Dying, are both alive and present, thus granting them greater control over language as well as procreation. Though the women generally pay a heavy price for refusing to deny their female sexuality, Faulkner ties that sexuality much more closely to maternity than in the previous texts, exploring a feminine creativity which is both maternal and sexual, literal and figurative, procreative and linguistic. Women's lives may be tied to their female bodies, but these women nevertheless reveal the precariousness of the definitions of gender which masculine culture produces and imposes. In so doing, they reveal masculinity for what it is: a fiction.

Chapter 5

Fantastic Women and Notmothers

Absalom, Absalom!

> It's much more fun to try to write about women because
> I think women are marvelous, they're wonderful, and I
> know very little about them, and so I just—it's much
> more fun to try to write about women than about
> men—more difficult, yes.
>
> *Faulkner in the University*

When considering *Absalom, Absalom!,* probably Faulkner's greatest achievement, one can well understand why he found women more fun to write about than men. Who could doubt that it would be more fun to create Rosa Coldfield than Quentin Compson, that Clytie is more "marvelous" than Henry Sutpen, and Eulalia Sutpen Bon more "wonderful" than Charles Bon? Faulkner's comment, however, reflects more than the entertainment value inherent in writing of women. His use of the terms "wonderful" and "marvelous" brings a particular aura to women, an aura that, when considered in the light of the women of *Absalom,* becomes uncannily fantastic.

Women in this novel are perceived as both real and unreal, both ordinary and extraordinary, both mothers and notmothers. While women with dual natures make frequent appearances in Faulkner's work, in other novels that duality tends to take on a more conventional and realistic aura, based on recognizable contradictions regarding the nature of femininity. Thus we encounter Caddy Compson moving between sister and mother, virgin and whore; Addie Bundren as mother and adulterer, dead body and speaking voice; Temple Drake with a body both boyish and evocative of feminine sexuality; Eula Varner who embodies virginity and fertility simultaneously; Lena Grove as asexual earth mother; Joanna Burden as sexually repressed nymphomaniac; Charlotte Rittenmeyer as a "better man" yet "profoundly feminine." Still, of all these examples of feminine duality, only Addie's ability to speak after death strains credulity, and given that Faulkner links this, through his title, to Homer, it becomes explainable through mythic associations.

In *Absalom,* however, the contradictory nature of women exceeds the bounds of conventional reality, aligning them with the mode of the fantastic, defined by Tzvetan Todorov as causing a hesitation while characters or readers try to decide whether the events stem from natural or supernatural causes. The inability to determine whether something is real or supernatural obliterates the boundaries between real and unreal and, in so doing, challenges their very existence. This erasure of boundaries, a function which corresponds to that of the mother, who elides the border between self and other, both collapses and enhances difference, making one intensely aware of the fluid boundaries between natural and supernatural, body and voice, individual and community. As Quentin Compson realizes of himself, "he was not a being, an entity, he was a commonwealth" (9). Individual autonomy, always shaky in Faulkner's fiction, becomes positively embattled by the combined force of the fantastic and the feminine, by women who take on an unworldly air in a world both intensively familiar and uncannily different.

Women, familiar creatures with fantastic dimensions, exemplify Faulkner's oxymoronic world, a familiar world made strange. In *Absalom, Absalom!,* a novel where questions of power and authority are so central, the presence of the women—and the fantastic nature of the women—attacks the dominant thematic and structural premises on which the novel rests. The result is a book which denies the very groundwork of its own authority, fictionalizing the Law of the Father yet also displacing the mother, for literal mothers are curiously absent, replaced by aunts; Rosa, her aunt, Judith, and Clytie overshadow Ellen, Eulalia, the octoroon, and Milly Jones. Maternal power is eerily transformed into a far more pervasive force, reaching beyond mothers and, for the first time in Faulkner's work, beyond white women as well.

In this, his most powerful novel, Faulkner confronts not just the feminine challenge to white patriarchy, but the racial challenge as well. Thomas Sutpen's dynasty goes down in flames in part because he fails to recognize daughters or racially mixed sons as potential heirs to his domain. However, Faulkner's most striking departure from his other work emerges in his presentation of important, interesting, and powerful African American women. While the theoretical racial questions, as always in Faulkner, are restricted primarily to male discussion and male concerns, the presence of Clytie and, to a lesser extent, of Eulalia and the octoroon highlights the bodily presence of racial difference, a difference which challenges white men and white women. Clytie, protector and avenger, figuratively embodies the forces which defeat white southern patriarchy and literally sets in motion the final stage of the fall of the house of Sutpen.

As the above cast of characters reveals, women, black or white, mothers or not, play a highly significant role in the novel. It is not surprising that a vast array of studies on the women of *Absalom* has replaced an era of criticism which focused almost exclusively on Quentin Compson and Thomas Sutpen.[1] Yet amid these many excellent essays, remarkably little has been said about the power of the mother—or, rather, the notmother—and her significance in a book haunted by ghostly and uncanny events. In fact, the lack of literal mothers may be the ghostliest and uncanniest concern of a novel in which obsession with the generation of family and anguish over individual autonomy hold such crucial positions. Quentin Compson may decide that he has too many fathers (his own, Shreve, and Thomas Sutpen) and Charles Bon that he has too few, but where are the mothers whose procreation creates the father?

The mother's literal absence is further enforced by the attempts of the male characters, and possibly Faulkner himself, to undermine maternal power by desubstantializing the women, for the ghostly aura associated with the feminine is born of and sustained by the perception of men. Just as the storytellers in *Absalom* create the fantastic nature of the tale by their perception of it, so the men of the novel often create the fantastic quality of the women through their tortured interpretations of the female psyche. Faulkner's authorial reticence in "explaining" his women leaves them open to the rather clumsy scrutiny of the men, who want them to submit quietly to their places in the patriarchal social order. When the women fail to do so, thereby threatening that order, the men attempt to dismiss them as unreal and thus to remove them from central consideration. By grabbing control of the tale and examining it in terms of father-son relationships,

Quentin and Shreve are able to glaze over the disturbing and ghostly attributes of Rosa's story. But the glaze does not quite take, because Faulkner has given the women enough power to counter the male dominance. The presence of the women not only defeats Sutpen's patriarchal design, but the voice—and silence—of the women denies the grounds of narrative authority on which the novel is based.

Rosa Coldfield, one of two women still alive at the point of the telling, is quickly shunted off into the realm of the supernatural. Her voice vanishes, she speaks in "notlanguage," and she appears to Quentin—and so to the reader—as a ghost. But Faulkner quite deliberately chains Rosa to the real world by her physical characteristics: she wears "eternal black," possibly for her "nothusband," and emits the "rank smell of female old flesh long embattled in virginity" (4). Through this description Rosa emerges as both physically present and figuratively absent, for she is defined by what she has not: husband and sexual experience. Yet we learn remarkably little about Rosa's appearance other than that she is composed of rank "female flesh" and is the size of a child. Though she has a body only insofar as it is female, virgin, and stunted, that body, represented as explicitly sexed, is all that separates her from ghostliness. Her physical reality rests on her sex and her lack of sexuality.

This linguistic dichotomy turns out to be a real dichotomy. She appears as both familiar and fantastic because she is not a natural woman but an unmarried woman emitting the "rank" smell of spinsterhood. By insisting on her virginal smell, Quentin not only distorts Rosa's personhood into spinsterhood, but paradoxically re-aligns her with maternity through the use of the sensual imagery which grounds her in the body. But Rosa, of course, is an aunt, not a mother. Devoid of sexual fulfillment and the social status of marriage, without a husband to define and control her, the maiden aunt holds a particularly marginal position in southern society, as Mr. Compson notes:

> Because that's what a Southern lady is. Not the fact that, penniless and with no prospect of ever being otherwise and knowing that all who know her know this, yet moving with a parasol and a private chamber pot and three trunks into your home . . . [she] not only takes command of all the servants . . . but goes into the kitchen and dispossesses the cook and seasons the very food you are going to eat to suit her own palate;—it's not this, not this that she is depending on to keep body and soul together: It is as though she were living on the actual blood itself like a vampire, not with

insatiability, certainly not with voracity, but with that serene and idle splendor of flowers abrogating to herself, because it fills her veins also, nourishment from the old blood that crossed uncharted seas and continents and battled wilderness hardships. (105)

Mr. Compson argues that poverty, lack of alternatives, and the pretence of domestic authority rank behind the allure of blood ties as reasons for a spinster to move in with her family. The maiden aunt keeps body and soul together not by pretending to be wife and mother (though his persuasive description certainly supports such a possibility) but by feeding off the family. She both usurps household authority and weakens the entire network of the family by sucking its blood. Though Mr. Compson tries to soften his vampire analogy by admitting that she may be neither insatiable nor voracious, such modifiers hold little sway over the powerful image he has just created. In Mr. Compson's eyes, the woman who fails to generate her own family is responsible for the undermining of the entire family framework; or, to put it more bluntly, the womb which should create and nourish is transformed by lack of use into a parasite which ultimately feeds off and destroys family life.

Furthermore, by the end of his comment, Mr. Compson has made it clear that family blood is patriarchal blood, representing founders who "crossed uncharted seas and continents" and passed on a "transmutable fountainhead" (105) to the next male descendent. The phallic imagery of the fountainhead evokes the experience of men, defining the family as male-centered and rendering the spinster even more marginal and problematic. In failing to serve as a receptacle of this "transmutable fountainhead," the notmother betrays both family and civilization. Where would America be if those uncharted seas and continents had not been crossed, if that "fountainhead" had not been passed on? Women's bodies are needed not to play at being wife and mother, but to fulfill those roles physically. A woman who does neither attacks both the immediate family, by feeding off it, and genealogical continuity, by refusing to nurture it. Both excluded from and imprisoned within family bonds, the powerless outsider paradoxically has the subversive force to undermine the household.

Rosa's case is particularly interesting, because she recognizes the patriarchal trap laid for unmarried women. Though patterned on Dickens's Miss Havisham, Rosa's situation stems not from a simple jilting but from the realization of what marriage will demand of her: to become a womb to bring forth men children only. It's unclear what prompts her to agree to marry Sutpen in the first place, a question she finds equally puzzling, admitting, "*I hold no brief for myself*" (198)—presumably, marriage to a demon is better than no marriage at all—but her outraged rejection follows his suggestion that they first breed to see if she will produce a male heir. One must conclude that Sutpen's blunt statement that she is wanted only to bear sons is what enrages her, not the suggestion of premarital sex, for when he first announces his decision to marry her, it seems as if the union will be immediately consummated without protest from her:

> He will decree this marriage for tonight and perform his own ceremony, himself both groom and minister; pronounce his own wild benediction on it with the very bedward candle in his hand: and I mad too, for I will acquiesce, succumb; abet him and plunge down. (206)

Yet that "plunge down" was only the simple act of sexual intercourse; the more pervasive insult lies in the brutal definition of her future role. This destruction of her romantic hopes and her corresponding realization that Sutpen's interest is only in her body and its potential as an incubator inspires Rosa to protect that body by becoming, in essence, a figurative vampire, not only ghoulishly feeding off the family by keeping herself alive on hatred but vigorously refusing to nurture a new family, refusing to accept the premise of wife as breeder or woman as body; she prefers her marginal, unconventional role as spinster, thereby hastening the collapse of the Sutpen dynasty and memorializing its downfall with the voice that refuses to cease, regardless of whether it vanishes.

Rosa's refusal to be a literal mother does not necessarily cut her off from maternal power. In fact, her mothering extends far beyond the children she might have borne. Rosa, in a sense, bears the novel. As John Matthews points out, Rosa's language creates both Thomas Sutpen and Charles Bon. "As creations of her language, they are represented by traces of their presence" (Matthews 132). She also, according to Rosemary Coleman, gives birth to Quentin Compson. "Rosa gives birth to Quentin by means of her summons to him; she fills him with her words; and then she uses him as the tool which she lacks" (428). Her mothering—or notmothering—is almost akin to fathering in its reliance on figurative creativity, and Coleman assigns Rosa the father's role in addition to the mother's: "Rosa is also, in a very real sense, the seminal father of the narrative as well" (Coleman 421). Certainly Rosa often seems to father the tale which Quentin carries to term in a book comprised of nine sections. But a notmother is not a father; Rosa indeed functions as the uncanny repository of self and notself, origin and other.

Consequently, Quentin, who attempts to separate from her with his almost frenzied insistence that she is not his aunt, ultimately abandons the effort. The novel's final reference to her shows Shreve calling her "the Aunt Rosa" without correction from Quentin.

> "And so it was the Aunt Rosa that came back to town inside the ambulance," Shreve said. Quentin did not answer; he did not even say, *Miss Rosa.* (468)

That Faulkner calls attention to Quentin's failure to correct Shreve suggests more than exasperated resignation to Shreve's teasing. Rather, Quentin seems finally to acknowledge his connection to, and even his re-engulfment in, his notmother, the woman who has birthed both the tale and his role as teller. John Irwin argues that Quentin's incestuous desires for Caddy in *The Sound and the Fury* constitute a desire to return to the womb, a wish for "the immersion of the masculine ego consciousness in the waters of its birth, in the womb of the feminine unconscious from which it was initially differentiated" (43). I would suggest that Rosa's *"lightless womb"* (179) is a more appropriate space for him than either the sister or the dungeon-mother of *Sound.* In fact, he may not need to return to the "lightless womb"; he may already be there.

It is difficult to determine, at times, where Quentin ends and Rosa begins. While he listens to her begin the tale, he splits into "two separate Quentins" (5); one of those Quentins, however, appears to become Rosa Coldfield, given the conversation—in "notlanguage"—the two have.

> *It seems that this demon—his name was Sutpen—(Colonel Sutpen)—Colonel Sutpen. Who came out of nowhere and without warning upon the land with a band of strange niggers and built a plantation—(Tore violently a plantation, Miss Rosa Coldfield says)—tore violently . . . and died. Without regret, Miss Rosa Coldfield says—(Save by her) Yes, save by her. (And by Quentin Compson) Yes. And by Quentin Compson.* (5–6)

While part of this dialogue maintains the illusion of two separate Quentins by its constant reminder—"Miss Rosa Coldfield says"—that one Quentin merely repeats Rosa's words, it is clear that Miss Rosa and this Quentin occasionally merge. Not only does their rhetoric sound the same, but we see Rosa intruding into Quentin's pschye and exerting enough influence to split his personality.

In addition, his being chosen as her listener marks him as inextricably linked to her story and her fate. Rosa claims to tell Quentin the tale because he is going away and not likely to return. "So I dont imagine you will ever come back here" (6). While she envisions a successful birth—he will separate and yet retain the trace of his origin and write about it some day—as we know from *Sound,* Quentin never will return, partly because he cannot separate, he cannot divide his identity from hers. He is tied to her by more than being "born and bred in the deep South the same as she was" (5). Both Quentin and Rosa share a tendency to evoke ghosts, a disturbed yearning for sexuality, a "crisis of lost love," as Matthews notes (132), and a desperate desire to believe that one can understand the South through telling, through language.

Despite, or because of, these similarities, Quentin's relationship with Rosa, unlike the one with Shreve, is no "happy marriage of speaking and hearing" (395). Rosa's language evokes a very different image for him. "It (the talking, the telling) seemed (to him, to Quentin) to partake of that logic- and reason-flouting quality of a dream which the sleeper knows must have occurred, stillborn and complete, in a second" (22). Comparing Rosa's narration to a "stillborn" dream does a vast disservice to the vibrant tale to which her language actually gives birth. Quentin's perception of it as "stillborn" says more of him than of her. It may be the ghostly quality of the creation which causes him to think of it as dead, but it may also have something to do with the listener himself. Quentin, in some ways, is born from this story, for it is the story of the South, the heritage which has created him. The stillborn dream, then, simultaneously suggests Thomas Sutpen, southern history, and Quentin Compson. If Quentin is stillborn of Rosa, he becomes a kind of "notson" to a notmother.

Rosa's uncanny relation to Quentin is, of course, rendered even more ghostly by the supernatural attributes associated with her, qualities imposed by Quentin and his father.[2] Quentin first characterizes her house as "coffin-smelling," sees the ghost "abrupt" out of "a quiet thunderclap" (4) in response to her voice, and senses that he's listening to a ghost "which had refused to lie still even longer than most had, telling him about old ghosttimes" (5). However, while Rosa may call Sutpen "fiend blackguard and devil" (14), her principal complaint of him is not that he is ghostly but that "he wasn't even a gentleman" (13). When Sutpen returns from the war with his suggestion that they produce a son before marrying, she draws back from her initial decision that he is mad. "*If he was mad, it was only his compelling dream which was insane and not his methods: it was no madman who bargained and cajoled hard manual labor out of men like Jones; it was no madman who kept clear of the sheets and hoods and night-galloping horses*" (207). Thus Rosa, despite the excess of her language, does not relinquish hold on reality, at least, not where Sutpen is concerned. She does not speak of the supernatural. Why, then, would Quentin identify her as a ghost who evokes ghosts?

The most obvious answer lies in his own genes. In many ways a chip off the old block, Quentin learns much from his father, particularly about women. Mr. Compson's first words in the novel reveal his desire to disembody the ladies.

> Years ago we in the South made our women into ladies. Then the War came and made the ladies into ghosts. So what else can we do, being gentlemen, but listen to them being ghosts? (10)

Presumably the destruction of southern hierarchy and chivalry turned the ladies into ghosts. Yet this whole network presumes a dominant male order. Mr. Compson sees the men as the prime movers: they turn the women into ladies, and, by losing the war, into ghosts who must be borne as the gentleman's burden. The male failure in the Civil War caused, the men hope, female disembodiment. Mr. Compson does not want to contemplate the possibility of women as a real presence once their men have been vanquished.

This eagerness to desubstantialize women also represents an attempt to erase the female body and its creative potential. Looking back to *Sound*, it makes sense that Mr. Compson would want to deny women's bodies, particularly that of his daughter, whose body procreates with deadly results for the family. Warwick Wadlington says of daughters in *Absalom*, "daughters tangle and knot a pure, straightforward patrilineage" (179). Daughters are wasted seed, bodies which go on to service a different patrilineage, become mothers to a different line. A daughter like Rosa who replaces her mother serves as "not only a living and walking reproach to her father, but a breathing indictment ubiquitous and even transferable of the entire male principle" (71). Pointing out the destructive and even murderous nature of "the entire male principle," daughters, like aunts, do not fit neatly into the line of patrilineal descent; in fact, their bodies are literal witnesses to the fragility of the line that dies out by producing daughters rather than sons. As Thomas Sutpen learns too late, it is not only the future of the male line which can be killed by the birth of daughters; Rosa refers to Milly Jones very accurately as *"the female flesh in which his name and lineage should be sepulchred"* (167). Indirectly, Sutpen finds his own body "sepulchred" in that "female flesh" as well. The presence of the female body thus taunts the men with a reminder of their failure and impotence.

Thus those bodies must be transformed, recast into ghosts, insects, or fleshless vessels. Rosa may become a ghost, but her sister Ellen suffers an even worse fate, as she becomes metamorphosed into a butterfly. Mr. Compson describes her as "the foolish unreal voluable preserved woman . . . [who] produced two children and then rose like a swamp-hatched butterfly, unimpeded by weight of stomach and all the heavy organs of suffering and experience" (83–84). Even her death contributes to her dehumanization:

> She had lost some flesh of course, but it was as the butterfly itself enters dissolution by actually dissolving: the area of wing and body decreasing a little, the pattern of spots drawing a little closer together, but with no wrinkle to show . . . the clinging moth, [who] even alive would have been incapable now of feeling anymore of wind or violence. (104)

Mr. Compson takes considerable pains to elaborate his simile, particularly to focus on its bodily aspects. Ellen seems to lose any sense of her human female body, "unimpeded by weight of stomach" and lacking the "organs of suffering and experience." Instead, he gives extended treatment to the "area of wing and body" and the "pattern of spots" on the body of the butterfly.

Ellen has lost more than her body; she has also lost that other defining human feature, her mind. She is "foolish" and "unreal," "incapable now of feeling." These assumptions deny human identity even more completely to her than to Rosa, for Rosa has a voice to counter the men's re-creation of her. Ellen, however, dead and silenced, is subjected to an "actual re-birth" (77), not of woman but of Jason Compson. Jenny Jennings Foerst links Mr. Compson's use of the butterfly imagery to the myth of Cupid and Psyche, claiming that "Psyche's final step towards individuation actively combats the *matriarchal*" (41) in its challenge of Aphrodite's maternal power. She goes on to argue that Mr. Compson attempts to define Ellen in matriarchal terms, albeit failed ones—she *"might* have risen to actual stardom in the role of the matriarch" (*AA* 83; my emphasis)—in order to deny her the erotic power of Psyche, who manages to defeat Aphrodite by marrying Cupid. Ellen, says Foerst, as well as her aunt, "escape to the state enabling the erotic, the state of matrimony" (Foerst 42). But this argument presumes that matriarchal power threatens patriarchy less than erotic power does. While true to some extent—sexual women are often regarded with fear and loathing in Faulkner's work—maternity confers a considerably greater threat. Mr. Compson may find comfort in the maternal definition not because it erases the erotic but because it is failed maternity.

Ellen, one of the few literal mothers presented in the novel, has her maternal power stripped away by the insistence on her lack of both mind and body. She produces two children; beyond that, she fails to serve as the anxious source of identity and engulfment, the position which the mother so often holds. Even her creative potential is dehumanized by the butterfly imagery, for butterflies, apparently, give birth to themselves, evolving out of cocoons. While Eula Varner's ability to birth herself may be interpreted positively, Ellen's falls short, for she births not herself but an insect, a male vision imposed on her. Her figurative "rebirth" leaves maternal power—and even humanity—behind. Like Temple Drake of *Sanctuary,* she is shunted off into the animal kingdom.

Cocoon imagery, in fact, occurs frequently in the novel, and not only in relation to Ellen. Rosa refers to Sutpen's Hundred as a *"cocoon-casket marriage-bed of youth and grief"* (168), created by Sutpen *"as the sweat of his body might have created, produced some (even if invisible) cocoon-like and complementary shell"* (172). She later describes the circumstances of the tradition into which Judith is nurtured as *"cocoon stages: bud, served prolific queen, then potent and soft-handed matriarch of old age's serene and well-lived content"* (194). Finally, Mr. Compson describes the octoroon similarly to Ellen:

> no human being . . . who would not grow from one metamorphosis—dissolution or adultery—to the next carrying along with her all the old accumulated rubbish-years which we call memory, the recognisable *I,* but changing from phase to phase as the butterfly changes once the cocoon is cleared, carrying nothing of what was into what is, leaving nothing of what is behind but eliding complete and intact and unresisting into the next avatar. (245–46).

The pervasiveness of this cocoon imagery offers a different kind of creative paradigm from either literal or figurative, maternal or patriarchal power. In its seemingly effortless and autonomous transformation, it relieves us of the need for mothers or fathers, thereby erasing gender as an element of procreation. But despite its apparent androgyny, it is a creativity more associated with men than women. Rosa identifies Sutpen's house as his cocoon, the house which he has engendered without female aid. Indeed, Sutpen himself makes every effort to transform himself from caterpillar to butterfly. On the other hand, Mr. Compson's imposition of cocoon imagery onto Ellen and the octoroon reveals a clear attempt to deny the creative power—and its implications—of women's bodies. It is surely no accident that both these women are mothers; one defuses maternal power by denying human identity to mothers. Cocoon creativity differs from maternal procreation in that it carries nothing forward and leaves nothing behind. Though Mr. Compson ascribes this state to the mothers, it applies even better to him and his son. A mode of creation which erases memory would free him from the burden of the past, from the reminders of his origin—in fact, from the mother.

It doesn't work, however. This novel is replete with various creative paradigms, and despite the attempts by both Mr. Compson and Rosa to erase sexual procreation, a mode they find particularly threatening, the cocoon cannot replace it. Memory, origin, is not so easily erased. Enough of Thomas Sutpen's mountain-boy past remains to prevent his understanding the complex permutations of class and race through anything other than the simplistic and inadequate analogy of the rifle. Even Quentin's initial vision of Sutpen's Hundred created by voice, "the *Be Sutpen's Hundred* like the oldentime *Be Light*" (5), is dispelled by the long description of the physical labor that went into creating that house out of the swamp and even by Sutpen's life story that explains the origins of his design. In each case, the body, the human body, cannot be denied. Sutpen's slaves may appear to the local populace as almost unearthly beings, believed to have the power "to actually conjure more cotton per acre from the soil than any tame ones had ever done" (87); they may rise out of the swamp like alligators, speaking "some dark and fatal tongue of their own" (41), but they have men's bodies and perform grueling manual labor. And Sutpen himself, though "looking as though [he] had been created out of thin air" (35), has a literal as well as a figurative origin. His mother provides "whatever slight hold the family had had . . . on the mountain (278), and her death thrusts him into an unfamiliar world of separation, as the father takes them to "a country all divided and fixed and neat" (276). He is born of woman, reborn through the mother's death, and reborn yet again by the insult to his appearance, to his unkempt body.

In fact, despite the rather desperate attempts to negate women's bodies, the only body truly erased is Thomas Sutpen's. His ghost haunts the novel, and his children destroy each other, leaving only "One nigger Sutpen left" (471), howling in the night, appropriately named Bond. Meanwhile, the women whom he insults, abuses, and takes for granted, live on not as ghosts, but "notghosts," fantastic beings who cannot be shuffled off into the realm of the supernatural, into which the men would place them. For their power is too great and too real. They are not simply listened to; they are believed and obeyed. Shreve sardonically notes that Rosa

> hadn't been out there, hadn't set foot in the house even in forty-three years, yet who not only said there was somebody hidden in it but found somebody that would believe her, would drive that twelve miles out there in a buggy at midnight to see if she was right or not? (221)

And she is absolutely right, which raises an interesting question: how did she know? For she not only knows something is out there, but that "It has been there for four years, living hidden in that house" (216). Who tipped her off? The strangers from Arkansas who are frightened away by some unexplained terror provide the only clue that something out of the ordinary may be lurking in that house. But because "*they did not or could not or would not tell*" (267) what happened, it seems unlikely that Rosa could have gotten her information from them. We must assume that some inexplicable feminine intuition enlightens her, the source of which appears to be otherworldly, since no force of this world could inform her. While Quentin, Shreve, and Mr. Compson spin out long and tortured explanations for the events surrounding the Sutpen men, they evince no interest in how Rosa gets her information, no concern for women's ways of knowing. Yet through its very existence, this mystery challenges "that best of ratiocination" (350), the best that masculine discourse has to offer.

Though Rosa, with her preference for "demonizing," may commune with the spirits, she still needs the help of a young man in carrying out the physical labor needed to accomplish her aim. But she does not rely on him too heavily, once again refuting the unworldly part of her nature. For when

Quentin drives her out to Sutpen's Hundred, he feels he knows her suffi-
ciently well now to predict what she will wear and bring.

> She would be wearing already the black bonnet with jet sequins; he knew
> that: and a shawl, sitting there in the augmenting and defunctive twilight;
> she would have all the keys, entrance closet and cupboard, that the house
> possessed . . . and a parasol, an umbrella too. (108)

A crucial detail is missing, however. Miss Rosa also carries a hatchet to
break into the house, something we discover only in the final pages.
Though she may have superhuman sources of knowledge, she does not
intend to float through the walls of the house without some practical aid.

Given the presentation of bodies in *Absalom,* she might well be able to
do so. Nancy Blake asserts that "Faulkner's text proceeds to destroy any
expectation of a body behind, beside, or underneath the all-powerful
name" (132). Women are particularly vulnerable: "Deficient in symbolic
presence, women in *Absalom* are either vehicles for the overpowering voice
or else evanescent images; they are, at all events, bodiless" (Blake 134).
Patrick O'Donnell, while arguing for the power of the body, still points out
that bodies in the novel "most often appear as forms in the process of
mutation: half-born, still-born, fluid, partial, intermingled with other bodies, commingled with the elements." He illustrates that even air, in many
passages, such as the one in which the octoroon "impregnates" the air of
her room "with the heavy fainting odor of her flesh, her days, her hours,
her garments" (*AA* 243), can take on a "fleshly aspect" (O'Donnell 30). If
bodies are so fluid that "the boundaries between flesh and the non-
corporeal are dissolute," as O'Donnell says, then Rosa would need no axe
to enter the house. Clearly, her body both has and erases boundaries, just
what one would expect from a notmother.

Her language displays similar dichotomies and complexities. Rosa, as
Judith Bryant Wittenberg points out, manipulates symbolic discourse quite
well, "not only as an instrument of creation but as a weapon of rebellion"
(100). Yet her language, Wittenberg claims, reveals "to what degree she is
caught in the genderized prisonhouse of language" (102). Her condemnation of her sister Ellen and her acceptance of dichotomies and categories
inscribe her within patriarchal discourse. Nonetheless, says Wittenberg,
"Rosa's refusal of either moderation or linearity can be seen as a form of
rebellion against the usual unfolding of patriarchal narrative" (104–05).
Minrose Gwin is not quite so positive, declaring that Rosa "is woman

trying to speak and coming to constitute the text of masculine madness" (66). Her language "deconstructs the very structures of its own feminist discourse" (Gwin 70).

These sometimes complementary and sometimes contradictory arguments reveal the complexity of Rosa's relation to and control over symbolic discourse. I would suggest that the difficulty of categorizing Rosa through a predominately Lacanian psychoanalytic model reveals its inadequacy for the task. As Faulkner recognized, the relation of body to language cannot always be classified or gendered, and while Kristeva's distinction between the semiotic and symbolic is often a useful tool for discussing his work, it can also fall short. In this novel, Rosa seems not so much to move between the two modes of discourse as to use them simultaneously. Her vanished voice, noted on the second page of the novel, emblemizes the collapse of both semiotic and symbolic, maternal and paternal language. Rosa's voice may vanish, but it does not cease: "Her voice would not cease, it would just vanish" (4). Rosa is not silenced, because voice is oral and so cannot be erased visually. Thus she remains within the symbolic realm.

Yet neither does she lose her body to this visual erasure, for her invisible voice can be linked to her female body. Women's language, to requote Luce Irigaray, "does not privilege sight; instead, it takes each figure back to its source, which is among other things *tactile*" (79). Quentin's erasure of Rosa's visibility then, through both losing sight of her voice and imposing ghostly attributes to her, puts her in touch with a feminine mode. It is Quentin who visualizes: the creation of Sutpen's Hundred and the scenes between Henry and Charles—"It seemed to Quentin that he could actually see them, facing one another at the gate" (164). In fact, he privileges his own visions above actual sight. *"If I had been there I could not have seen it this plain"* (238). Rosa, on the other hand, emphasizes what she does not see: "But I was not there. I was not there to see the two Sutpen faces this time—once on Judith and once on the negro girl beside her—looking down through the square entrance to the loft" (33). Though Rosa here uses vision similarly to Quentin in that she vividly presents what she does not actually see, she also focuses more on her exclusion—"I was not there"— than her inclusion, subtly highlighting her distance from the scene by its emphasis on the two *Sutpen* faces.

She also recasts vision in her vicarious love for Charles Bon whom she has never seen, and whom, perhaps, she loves because she has never seen him. She does not need to see him because *"even before I saw the photograph*

I could have recognised, nay, described, the very face" (183). While Quentin's vision is born of words, of storytelling, Rosa's grows out of the physical presence of Charles Bon in her house. "[I]*t was as though that casual pause at my door had left some seed, some minute virulence in this cellar earth of mine"* (181). Thus despite her statement that she lives this "*miscast summer . . . not as a woman, a girl, but rather as the man which I perhaps should have been"* (179), her imagery suggests that, in fact, she gives birth to the vision of Charles Bon. Once his "seed" comes to term in her "cellar earth," she can see his face without needing the photograph. Erasing neither the visual nor the tactile, neither the semiotic nor the symbolic, Faulkner opens up a space between gendered discourse, a place where Rosa can indeed become "*all polymath love's androgynous advocate"* (182).

Rosa may feel she becomes love's "androgynous advocate," and that she perhaps should have been a man, but the novel would have lost considerable force had Faulkner agreed with her. Her engendering voice grants her a power unknown to any other woman in his fiction, and it is a power explicitly feminine yet separated from maternity, for Rosa is emphatically not a mother. What we see in *Absalom* is not so much the power of the mother as the power of the notmother, often configured as the aunt. The displacement of maternal power onto the aunt, particularly given the compelling portrait of Sutpen as failed father, strikes a strange imbalance within the family. In splitting off literal procreative power from uncanny maternal power, Faulkner seems to be trying to deny the full creative potential of the mother. Rosa, who, among all his women characters has the strongest voice, must be denied literal procreative power. Even more than Joanna Burden or Charlotte Rittenmeyer, a Rosa who bore children would overshadow even Thomas Sutpen to become the imaginative center of the book. Or maybe she already has, and to make her into a mother would somehow limit her disruptive potential. As it is, she functions as a source both of negation, in her refusal to bear Sutpen sons, and productivity, in her originating the tale itself.

In fact, Rosa negates more than Sutpen continuity, as her presence in the book denies narrative as well as family lines. Her second monologue, which comprises section five, does very little to advance the plot, that is, if we read the plot as the Henry/Charles conflict. The monologue is placed directly after Wash Jones's announcement that Henry has just "shot that durn French feller. Kilt him dead as a beef" (165). Now this is the episode which Quentin and Shreve want to investigate—why Henry shoots

Charles. But Faulkner negates their plot and tale by interposing Rosa's long monologue between the event and their next attempts to fathom it, resulting in a denial of the terms many critics have employed, a denial that the shooting is the central conflict. By including Rosa's section and by its placement, Faulkner suggests that Rosa's concerns are just as central—for this is indeed the physical center of the text—as Quentin's. Thus he denies the entire notion of centrality, the patrilineal tradition of the dominance of one line, be it genealogical or authorial. But this placement also opens up tremendous potential for multiple readings of the novel by erasing the dominance of any one perspective. Rosa's personal story challenges Sutpen's design, the patriarchal family, and men's ways of seeing.

It also challenges woman's role as mother, for Rosa finds herself paired with two more aunts, whether she realizes this or not. As might be expected, their relationship evokes both sameness and separation.

> I had for company one woman whom, for all she was blood kin to me, I did not understand and, if what my observation warranted me to believe was true, I did not wish to understand, and another who was so foreign to me and to all that I was that we might have been not only of different races (which we were), not only of different sexes (which we were not), but of different species, speaking no language which the other understood. (191)

Yet three pages later she describes the three of them as *"one being, interchangeable and indiscriminate"* (194). Both different and "one being," the three seem to function as mothers to each other, offering symbiotic union and autonomy. Yet because they are not mothers but aunts, the dichotomy lacks the threat that maternal duality generally inspires. This community of aunts, from Rosa's perspective, rather than bonding together simply lives together; they sleep in the same room for safety rather than companionship, share out the work *"with no distinction among the three of us of age or color but just as to who could build this fire or stir this pot . . . with the least cost to the general good in time or expense of other duties"* (193–94). The differences among them are mental, while the sameness means working together for the common good. In this endeavor, they lose both race and gender, living *"not as two white women and a negress, not as three negroes or three whites, not even as three women, but merely as three creatures who still possessed the need to eat . . . and in whom sex was some forgotten atrophy"* (193).

This is no egalitarian vision of the collapse of difference, for what Rosa primarily denies is the body, the site on which sexual and racial difference is inscribed as the determination of human identity. The erasure of race and gender comes about as the result of the physical erasure rather than through any sudden humanitarian enlightenment. She negates the body because of its atrophied sex; in a world without men, one becomes essentially sexless and thus undifferentiated. With the death of Charles Bon—and thus of love—Rosa seems to find no further use for the body other than as a carrying case for human life. Until Sutpen's brutal definition of her body as a son-making machine, she does not seem to contemplate maternity as connected to sexual love, focusing on the romantic and erotic rather than the procreative power of the body. In fact, Rosa's use of womb imagery reflects her identification of the womb as stagnant, destructive rather than creative. She describes her early life as *"that unpaced corridor which I called childhood, which was not living but rather some projection of the lightless womb itself"* (179). The "lightless womb" envelops the "notliving," a combination which challenges women's creative power, for the womb, source of feminine creation, does not nourish and produce; it seems to engulf rather than exude life.

This fear of the womb makes sense in Rosa, a child "born, at the price of her mother's life and never . . . permitted to forget it" (70). The importance of her birth lies in death rather than life, leaving her with a lifelong guilt and consequent hostility toward and fear of becoming a mother. Her own mother's death during childbirth suggests an incomplete birth; while the image is not quite as strikingly presented as the birth of Pilate in Toni Morrison's *Song of Solomon* where the baby emerges *after* the mother's death, Rosa nonetheless seems to suffer from never having been fully born. Thus she lives *"in that womb-like corridor where the world came not even as living echo but as dead incomprehensible shadow"* (202). Linda Wagner-Martin examines Rosa as spurned daughter, noting the similarities in fathering between Goodhue Coldfield and Thomas Sutpen. Rosa suffers equally from the lack of a mother; she has been "aunted" rather than mothered, and remains, in some ways, a child all her life. Her body never takes on its full adult stature, and she never contemplates becoming a mother herself, never having seen the potential power inherent in that position.

Without the power of maternity, she allows herself to be inscribed by the community, a fact of which she is well aware, constantly repeating to Quentin, "they will have told you." In fact, her frequent repetition of this assumption may reveal some pride in being figuratively constructed by the community, for verbal creativity does not threaten her the way physical procreation does. (In fact, she spends the war writing patriotic verse as a rebellion against her pacifist father.) Yet amid all her claims of what they will and will not have told, she interestingly omits the telling of the insult itself. *"It can be told; I could take that many sentences, repeat the bold blank naked and outrageous words just as he spoke them"* (208). But she does not; it is Shreve who finally articulates Sutpen's suggestion. The omission may be Quentin's rather than Rosa's, but given that this section does not come to us through his perspective as section one does, it seems, rather, to be Faulkner's. By not allowing her to verbalize it, Faulkner illustrates that the words do not constitute the true insult. Her real gripe with Sutpen lies *"not so much for the saying of it but for having thought it about her"* (214). Language is thus relegated to a simple system of expression, not the Biblical creativity Quentin envisions. By privileging the unspoken, Rosa refutes the ability of verbal discourse to define her bodily function, further negating Sutpen's symbolic power by not re-uttering, not recreating his words. In refusing to bear either his babies or his language, she refuses the role of maternal vessel. The Thomas Sutpen she births through her language is *her* Sutpen, not Sutpen as he conceives himself. Rosa thus appropriates creativity that negates both literal and symbolic, a creativity which takes on an aura of "notbirthing." Though she immortalizes Sutpen through her telling, it is an immortality based on her terms, her definitions.

Similarly, her niece Judith memorializes her father not by bearing his heirs, but by honoring his unacknowledged descendents with tombstones, recasting the Sutpen family through her own actions rather than those of her father. Like her father, Judith buys the stones even before some of them die, an act which baffles Mr. Compson. While he views with amused tolerance Sutpen's smuggling of the tombstones for himself and Ellen in the midst of the war, through the Yankee blockade and the Confederate army, he finds Judith's purchase of two more stones for Charles Bon and his son considerably more disturbing, remarking, "They lead beautiful lives—women. Lives not only divorced from, but irrevocably excommunicated from, all reality" (240). Why does a similar action provoke such a statement when a woman performs it? Why should Judith's motivations be so much more mysterious than Sutpen's? The answer, I think, lies in what those tombstones mean. Sutpen wants to increase the grandeur of his

dynasty by immortalizing the founders. This egotistical self-aggrandize-
ment makes perfect sense to Mr. Compson; even if he does not fully
approve of the gesture, he can sympathize with Sutpen's obsession with
genealogy. What Mr. Compson cannot explain is why Judith would provide a tombstone for the man who helped to destroy that dynasty. The
establishment of a patriarchal order is a "real" event, and because Judith's
action fails to celebrate that establishment—and, in fact, celebrates the
agent of its downfall—Mr. Compson must deny it any "real" meaning. He
accomplishes that denial by removing women's lives and motivations from
the realm of reality. What does not serve the patriarchal order must not
exist in the "real" world.

Judith's anti-patriarchal stance seems largely ignored by the men of the
novel. Mr. Compson suggests that Charles Bon sees in Judith "merely the
shadow, the woman vessel with which to consummate the love whose
actual object was the youth" (133). This privileging of homoeroticism over
heterosexuality implies a distrust of women, not of heterosexuality, for Mr.
Compson does not envision homosexuality; love will be consummated in
the "woman vessel." But true emotional commitment is between men, not
between men and women. Judith is "just the blank shape, the empty vessel
in which each of them strove to preserve, not the illusion of himself nor his
illusion of the other but what each conceived the other to believe him to
be" (148). This "empty vessel" contains not death colored menstrual blood
as in *Light in August* but male imaginative fantasies, the image of what
each man "conceived the other to believe him to be," implying figurative
rather than literal creativity. That blank shape, however, serves a physical
purpose as well, in another opinion expressed by Mr. Compson, but
attributed to Charles Bon. "[A] woman's sole end and purpose [is] to love,
to be beautiful, to divert" (145). By recasting her as a vessel of figurative
creativity and defining her physical body as erotic rather than maternal,
Mr. Compson denies her the uncanny power of maternity, identifying the
womb as an incubator rather than a source of life. However Judith defeats
all expectations, becoming not mother nor lover nor empty vessel of
imaginative fantasy, as Henry and Charles are forced to break through the
illusions and confront each other as they truly are: similarly descended but
racially different.

To Quentin and Shreve, Judith appears not as a vessel but as a failed
"notwoman," denied both the erotic and the maternal. She becomes "*the
spinster in homemade and shapeless clothing, with hands that could either*

transfer eggs or hold a plow straight in a furrow" (233). Her "shapeless"
clothes may fit a body presented as a "blank shape," but by calling her
spinster they deny her sensual or sexual power. A vessel no longer, she
now uses femininity in a rather peculiar way, as the boys conceive it. They
picture her talking to Charles Etienne and advising him to put aside his
black wife, *"her voice soft and swooning, filled with that seduction, that
celestial promise which is the female's weapon: 'Call me Aunt Judith, Charles'"*
(261). Why would she call upon seductive powers to claim her status as
aunt? First of all, we have no way of knowing whether or not Judith knows
of her relation to Charles Bon. The boys may imply that she uses the term
not in recognition of the actuality but in an effort to assert a closer tie to
Charles Etienne and thus gain greater control over him. But whether or
not she realizes the connection matters little in this case, for the use of a
seductive voice interferes with either possibility. It seems that Quentin and
Shreve find themselves unable to imagine a woman using persuasive powers without relying on seduction. Yet in associating aunts and seduction
they do highlight the unusually provocative power which aunts exert in the
novel.

Still, this entire scene comes from the storytelling of Quentin and
Shreve. There is no evidence whatsoever that Judith is even disturbed by
Charles Etienne's marriage. All we know of her relations with him is that
she and Clytie go to considerable trouble to track him down after his
mother dies, provide him with a home, and nurse him in his sickness, at
the cost of Judith's life. The picture of Clytie scrubbing away at the
"smooth faint olive tinge from his skin," and of Judith's hands which
"seemed at the moment of touching his body to lose all warmth and
become imbued with cold implacable antipathy," are sheer fabrication
(248). Having constructed a story in which men play the primary roles,
they define the relationships among these three on the premise that
Charles Etienne suffers emotional abuse from his two aunts. The aunts'
coldness emphasizes their difference from his mother, the woman who
exudes a "passionate and inexorable hunger of the flesh" (242). Aunts, the
boys seem to believe, lack such connection to the flesh and thus try to deny
the body, losing warmth at physical touch and erasing skin color. The
aunt's erotic power is verbal, not physical.

Judith, however, does recognize the importance of the physical. In
giving Bon's letter to Mrs. Compson, she demonstrates a desire to preserve
the physical evidence of his existence, much as she does in buying the

tombstones. The stone continues the life that has ceased to exist in the flesh. She replaces the body with a stone "because it never can become *was* because it cant ever die or perish" (158). If Judith here comes across as beaten, a very different woman from the child who insisted on racing the horses and watched unmoved as her father beat his slaves bloody and senseless, it is Sutpen's pursuit of patriarchal descent which has defeated her. Yet those tombstones constitute her final revenge against the design which has destroyed her life and the lives of her brothers by eternalizing its death. The body may become "was," but the celebration of the death of the body—and through it, the dynasty—will never perish. She manages to transform her father's figurative family line into literal tombstones.

In refusing to play the role of the grieving widow/sister, Judith further denies the importance of the patriarchal plot. Leslie Heywood writes that "Judith's insisting that 'it doesn't matter' is her way of exposing the groundlessness of the phallogocentric world which purports to fix and inscribe meaning through the hierarchical constructions it uses to order the world" (18). Judith denies the fixity of meaning on which phallogocentrism is grounded, both in her refusal to accept the terms of patriarchal family structure and also in her own fluid identity. Mr. Compson sees her as blank shape and erotic body; Quentin and Shreve perceive her as a sexless, seductive spinster; Rosa views her as inexplicable and unknowable. This ever-changing characterization aligns her, despite her lack of procreation, with the maternal ability to erode clear distinctions and divisions.

Given these powerful and maternal aunts, who needs mothers? Indeed, it appears that the plethora of aunts in this novel begins to crowd out the mother, most obviously in the example of Mr. Coldfield's sister, the aunt who arranges Ellen's wedding and raises Rosa until climbing out of the window and disappearing to get married. We first hear of this aunt through her role in setting up the wedding, persuading Mr. Coldfield to go along with it and then, when it looks like no one will come, going through the town calling on people "not to invite [them] to a wedding but to dare [them] not to come" (64).

The aunt's role raises a fascinating question: where is Ellen's mother? She is not dead, for Rosa has not yet been born. Why, then, is she never mentioned in relation to her daughter's wedding? The only references to her in the book reiterate her death in childbirth, and her absence in what should be a significantly important moment—the marriage of her eldest (and, at this point, only) daughter—is profoundly disturbing. One can easily conceive of Mrs. Coldfield as quiet and submissive, allowing her sister-in-law to take control of the household and childrearing, but that she does not even warrant a mention undermines any such rational supposition. If she has a recognizable role, it needs to be mentioned. Yet no one in the novel remarks on her absence, and while one cannot rule out a simple mistake on Faulkner's part (he may have thought of her as already dead), one still has to speculate on a possible meaning for it. By erasing the mother even before her death, Faulkner subtly highlights maternal absence in a book obsessed with fathers. It may be that paternal failure is linked to such absence, for fathering is not a singular act, literally or symbolically.

Robert Con Davis argues that "the question of the father in fiction, in whatever guise, is essentially one of father absence" (3). *Absalom*, however, has no absent fathers. Though Charles Bon may suffer from paternal absence as a child, we meet him in the novel just as he discovers his father. What's missing in the book are mothers: the mother of Ellen and Rosa, Quentin's mother, and even Bon's mother, who is only reconstructed through the boys' language, which we are never sure is an accurate rendition. Davis goes on to state that "the initial absence of the father inaugurates a desire for the father's function" (7). John Irwin, tracing the psychological implications of the doublings and repetitions which Quentin confronts, notes that Quentin uses his control of the tale as part of his struggle against his father.

> For Quentin, the act of narrating Sutpen's story, of bringing that story under authorial control, becomes a struggle in which he tries to best his father, a struggle to seize "authority" by achieving temporal priority to his father in the narrative act. (114)

But reading the narrative struggle as an analogue for an oedipal struggle entrenches narrative authority as paternal authority. Quentin may take on the father's function, his father being not literally absent but, to some degree, symbolically absent. Yet there are other absent functions in this book, functions equally important as narrative control. Does the absence of the mother "inaugurate a desire" for the mother's function?

Quentin's final intuitive leap seems to bear this out. His interview with Clytie, and, as far as we know, with Henry, offers no concrete information regarding the final piece of the puzzle, Charles Bon's African American ancestry. Shreve says of Clytie, "she didn't tell you in the actual words because even in the terror she kept the secret; nevertheless she told you, or at least all of a sudden you knew—" (438). This information is not told in "actual words." Quentin's enlightenment appears to come from a combination of intuition and reading in Clytie's body the possibility of another mixed-race Sutpen. By recognizing the importance of bodies, and by his possible ability to obliterate physical boundaries and melt into her consciousness, both modes associated with maternity, Quentin comes to his final conclusion, his ultimate fiction. He may "best his father" in the struggle for narrative authority, but he must rob the mother, appropriate her power, to bring his tale to term.

Quentin is not the only seeker and thief of maternal creativity. The women, particularly the aunts, the notmothers, also take over her role. Just as the father's role exceeds literal paternity, so does the mother's, allowing notmothers a piece of the action as the maternal power to create and obliterate self, to assert sameness and difference, resonates throughout the book. The scant number of mothers seems to unleash a powerful maternal force. Thus Ellen's aunt, "twice the man that Mr Coldfield was," becomes "not only Miss Rosa's mother but her father too" (75). When maternal power is not limited to literal mothers, not confined within a body which has borne children, it usurps even the paternal function, taking maternal duality beyond a merging of sameness and difference, self and other, to a collapse of feminine and masculine.

No character embodies this duality more than Clytie, "without sex or age" (169), another aunt, though largely unrecognized as such, due to her race. In fact, Clytie lacks recognition as aunt, as woman, and even as having been born, since she "never possessed" age. When Rosa hears Clytie's voice, she says, "it was as though it had not been she who spoke but the house itself that said the words—the house which he had built, which some suppuration of himself had created about him" (172). Rosa thus identifies Clytie as "some suppuration" of Sutpen, and, indeed, many of Clytie's actions in protecting the family bear this out. As Loren F. Schmidtberger has established, Clytie may be very well aware of the full situation. Mr. Compson notes that "no one but your grandfather and perhaps Clytie ever [knew] that Sutpen had gone to New Orleans too" (85). Clytie, as Schmidtberger points out, may well have learned of Sutpen's first wife from her mother and the other slaves who came from Haiti; thus she makes an obvious confidant for Sutpen (Schmidtberger 257). When she keeps people away from Charles Etienne, she may be preventing anyone from questioning him closely and thus learning the story through him (Schmidtberger 260). Susan Donaldson notes that she also effectively prevents Henry from telling the story by setting fire to the house, to him, and to herself (Donaldson 29).

While Clytie certainly appears to protect the Sutpen family, thus taking on the father's function, whether she actively contributes to her father's design is questionable. "Her position in the narrative," says Thadious Davis, "challenges conventional mechanisms contrived for identifying family members and for defining the 'central I-Am' of the individual" (199–200). She revises the definition of family and self with her refusal to open herself up to narrative analysis and her insistence that, despite her slave status, she is a literal member of the family, erasing the laws which deny her legal existence as a Sutpen. Her actions also de-father the family in that her loyalty lies not so much to Sutpen as to her half-brother and -sister, with whom she apparently lives on terms of harmony. More importantly, Clytie stands for everything that destroys Sutpen's design. As Rosa points out,

> the very pigmentation of her flesh represented that debacle which had brought Judith and me to what we were and which had made of her (Clytie) that which she declined to be just as she had declined to be that from which its purpose had been to emancipate her, as though presiding aloof upon the new, she deliberately remained to represent to us the threatful portent of the old. (195)

Far from existing as "some suppuration" of Sutpen's, his downfall—and that of the South—is inscribed on her body. Clytie's racial status reminds Rosa of slavery and miscegenation, the latter a devastating consequence of the former.

Interestingly, except for Rosa, no one views her mixed blood as particularly threatening; as a woman, she cannot compete for primogeniture, disqualified by gender rather than race. Yet it is precisely because she lacks the disruptive power of a Joe Christmas or a Charles Bon that she represents, in far more complex ways, the "debacle" of the Sutpen family. By failing to identify miscegenation as a problem when it occurs in women, the South tacitly denies that racial mixing holds a position of chief cultural concern. Denying anxiety to racial identity denies the very issue for which Thomas Sutpen repudiates his first wife and son, the very issue for which Henry Sutpen kills his brother. Thus Clytie's existence and position uncover the lack of logic at the core of southern notions of segregation and racial purity and denies them universal status.

Clytie further challenges the power of racial definition by remaining aloof from her racial status. She "declines" to be defined as either black or white. This translates also into declining to be defined by her father or her mother, the sources of her mixed blood. Rosa's closing words, however, leave the power with the mother's side. "Aloof" from the new, Clytie represents the "threatful portent of the old." The language speaking for black female identification as a threatful portent overpowers her aloof presiding over her father's whiteness. As Donaldson argues, "One of the most silent characters in the text as a whole, her very presence serves to contradict the 'forensic' and 'oratorical' swaggering upon which Thomas Sutpen relies to define himself and his patriarchal design" (30). Her presence also makes vivid the reminder of the black mother, both her own and Eulalia Bon. In fact, I would suggest that Clytie is what Dilsey is not: a powerful black mother.

It is plausible to believe that, as the eldest (and a girl) of the three children at the Hundred, she may very well have taken on some of the mothering of the younger two, particularly given her status as servant and their weak mother. But unlike Dilsey's situation, Clytie's subservient status does not seem to enter in to her relations with Henry and Judith, as she sleeps either in the bed or on the pallet with Judith, who certainly treats her with the respect lacking in the Compson children for Dilsey. Like Dilsey, she defends Henry and Judith with her words and with her body, but does so much more effectively and without apparent self-abnegation. Her voice and her hand prevent Rosa from intruding on Judith's privacy, and she exerts both again to protect Henry from a similar intrusion. She "overtook Miss Coldfield and caught her arm and said, 'Don't you go up there, Rosie' and Miss Coldfield struck the hand away and went on toward the stairs" (460).

Now old and frail, without Judith's voice to support her, Clytie fails in this attempt, but the effort matches her earlier successful one. Even here, she asserts her equality with her brother and sister: "Whatever he done, me and Judith and him have paid it out" (461). This is no self-denying mammy saying hit me instead of hitting Miss Quentin; this is a woman who defines herself not racially but familially and who celebrates that identity in protecting the family. While her identification with Henry and Judith remains problematic, like Ringo's identification with the Sartorises in *The Unvanquished,* it does refute race as a determining characteristic of human identity. Rosa may find Clytie *"incapable of freedom,"* but this results from her *"never once call[ing] herself a slave"* (195). By asserting control over her own identity, Clytie frees herself to identify as and with whom she chooses.

A sister/mother like Caddy Compson, Clytie stands in an even more interesting position to Rosa. Though Rosa calls her sister, either in recognition of Charles Bon's identity or on the assumption that Clytie, too, is in love with Bon, Clytie functions more as a mother than a sister to Rosa. Rosa herself describes Clytie's restraining arm as a *"fierce rigid umbilical cord"* and recognizes Clytie's touch as intruding upon her inmost being, *"the citadel of the central I-Am's private own"* (173). Minrose Gwin points out that Rosa denies herself in denying Clytie. Rosa's demand, *"Take your hand off me, nigger!"* (173), erases the one person who does her *"more grace and respect than anyone else I knew"* by recognizing that she was *"no child"* (172). "When Rosa rejects Clytie, she invalidates herself as a full, caring, significant woman—as the *Rosa* of Clytie's defining voice" (Gwin 87).

In this power both to define and to negate Rosa, Clytie perfectly fills the role of the spectral mother, as Madelon Sprengnether defines it, whose body functions "as a locus of difference and estrangement" (233). Unable to accept Clytie as origin, even though she has recognized that Clytie emblemizes the debacle of the South which has created them all, Rosa is cut off from any hope of erasing her primal loss, the death of her biological mother in giving birth to her, and cut off from any possibility of redeeming maternity. Rosa does become, in some ways, "one of the boys," as Gwin says, in denying Clytie (86). Clytie's role as primal mother of the tale goes unrecognized, victim to the racism which destroys the old patriarchal order and the Sutpens. And with that loss also flees any hope of reconciling self and other, home and not home: for Rosa, for Quentin, and for the South.

Thus Mr. Compson's assumption that Sutpen erred in naming Clytie— "I have always liked to believe that he intended to name her Cassandra, prompted by some pure dramatic economy not only to beget but to designate the presiding augur of his own disaster, and that he just got the name wrong" (74)—reveals that he has less understanding than Sutpen of her role. Cassandra uses words, predicts the truth that no one will believe. It is Rosa who has "an air Cassandralike and humorless and profoundly and sternly prophetic" (22), as she identifies the doom of the South—its failure to accept Clytie—in words that no one, not even she, can truly believe. Clytie, however, eschews language for action; if she provides words to Quentin, it is because he has finally learned how to read her body, how to come to recognize maternal rather than symbolic discourse.

Clytemnestra, a far more powerful woman, who murders her husband upon his return from war, partly in revenge for his earlier sacrifice of their daughter, serves as a much more accurate role model for Clytie herself. Clytie may not murder Sutpen on his return, but she doesn't need to; what she represents has already effectively killed off his design. Rather than being murdered by the son as was the original Clytemnestra, Clytie revises the plot, murdering Henry when she burns the house down. Finally, as Thadious Davis points out, like her namesake, she vanquishes Cassandra/Rosa "because she finally thwarts Rosa's efforts to control the Sutpens by taking charge of Henry" (205). She thereby erases the entire Sutpen/Coldfield clan, leaving behind only Jim Bond, the mulatto heir, to mark the final dissolution of white patriarchal authority and continuity. Rosa may father the tale but Clytie re-engulfs it, leaving behind the howling which Quentin still hears, and the ashes out of which it will rise again like a phoenix, rebirthing itself from a novel which bestows maternal creative power on those who tell it and those who read it.

Shreve says of women, "you cant beat them: you just flee" (389). But given the mother's power over origin, that umbilical cord which never seems definitively to be broken, you generally end up back where you started. Thus Henry Sutpen comes home to die in the house that created him and with the woman who mothered him. Thus Quentin Compson elects, in a novel already written, to engulf himself in water, to erase his primal separation through death. Thus Thomas Sutpen finds himself "sepulchred" in female flesh, returned to the "lightless womb" itself. Each of these characters is re-engulfed by the power of the notmother, an emblem of origin and difference, semiotic and symbolic, mother and father and aunt all in one.

It now becomes even more clear why these men try to redefine women as ghosts. With their uncanny power to control the fates of men, notmothers defy and deny the patriarchal ordering of the world. In no other novel does Faulkner present such a powerful maternal challenge. The book ends with the house of Sutpen literally destroyed and with Quentin frantically reiterating that he doesn't hate the South, recalling his earlier insistence that Rosa is not his aunt. Indeed she is not; she is something immensely more powerful: a rival creator of fictions, a woman with the power to disembody him, a notmother whose creativity he must rob to complete his tale of the fall of the patriarchal design. Like his creator, he has learned that the storyteller, the writer, will not hesitate to rob the mother.

Reading Faulkner's work through the paradigm of his figurative theft helps to clarify the intimate connections between physical and linguistic creative power. Long celebrated for his stylistic sophistication and the virtuosity of his prose, Faulkner is also an author who anticipates some of the physical sensationalism of contemporary literature, vividly portraying rape, castration, abortion, and murder, and thus forcing the body into the forefront of the text. Creativity, even linguistic creativity, must be embodied, as he highlights the tension between figurative and literal, illustrating how their intersection merges the limitations and possibilities of each. In collapsing these distinctions by collapsing gender, he implicitly erases the dichotomies so often set up in his fiction: bodies and language, individual and community, present and past, black and white, innocence and experience. Boundaries are transgressed through the force of maternal fluidity.

Maternal power, while not restricted to literal mothers, tends, not surprisingly, to be exerted by women. Though the relative importance of the roles of women in Faulkner's novels varies, and though the female characters themselves are generally silenced, exiled, or killed off, the psychological impact of women's bodies exerts a powerful force. Despite the literal absences of Caddy Compson and Addie Bundren, their bodies control the plots of their respective texts. Temple Drake and Eula Varner may function as commodities in a male-dominated culture, but the vivid presence of their sexuality mocks and destroys male illusions of potency and power and thus forces a realization that the nature of humanity rests on respecting women's bodies. While *Light in August* ostensibly divides sexuality and maternity, both Lena Grove and Joanna Burden manage to operate within literal and symbolic discourse, denying even the structural division which the novel attempts to impose on them. Likewise, though maternity itself seems divided and defeated in *The Wild Palms,* with Charlotte rejecting her life-giving potential at the literal cost of her own life and the pregnant-woman-turned-mother reduced to a "monstrous [barely] sentient womb," the impact of maternal power defines and controls men's lives. Finally, in *Absalom, Absalom!* Faulkner recasts the mother as the notmother, as maternal creativity transcends the boundaries of bodies, of language, and of race.

From *The Sound and the Fury,* where the Compson sons find themselves unable to escape the engulfment of the feminine, to *Absalom, Absalom!,* where Quentin and Rosa successfully employ maternal creativity to deliver his greatest novel, Faulkner testifies to the mother's function as a source of creative power. Whether or not mothers are literally present, their influence shows in the struggle between literal and figurative discourse, between bodies and language. Given her position as origin and other, she challenges the move into individual autonomy. Identity and language, both "meagre and fragile threads" in Faulkner's work, must be established via their relation to the Mother—real or symbolic. Yet in confronting the fragility of boundaries and identity, in recognizing that language provides no refuge from the body, Faulkner's novels both celebrate and challenge the art of fiction. Figurative creativity is inextricably linked to literal procreative power, granting it a compelling physical presence which envelops characters and readers alike.

Notes

Chapter 1

1. Noel Polk offers one of the first treatments of the mother in "'The Dungeon Was Mother Herself.'" But he looks more closely at the sons' reactions to her than at the nature of maternal power.

Chapter 2

1. David Minter, one of the exceptions, points to a failure of both parents and links that failure to Faulkner's mixed emotions toward his own parents, especially his supportive but domineering mother. He asserts that Faulkner's sympathy lies with children in both this novel and *As I Lay Dying* (97). For condemnations of Mrs. Compson see Cleanth Brooks, *The Yoknapatawpha Country* (333–34); Mark Spilka, "Quentin Compson's Universal Grief" (456); Jackson J. Benson, "Quentin Compson: Self-Portrait of a Young Artist's Emotions" (148); Elizabeth Kerr, "The Women of Yoknapatawpha" (94). Brooks offers one of the more sympathetic treatments of Mr. Compson. While Mrs. Compson has been the subject of fewer diatribes in recent criticism, in general the critical tendency seems to be to judge her while analyzing her husband, thus implicitly granting him a more privileged position.

2. Philip Weinstein also discusses Caroline Compson in a fine essay, "'If I could Say Mother,'" which I first saw after this chapter was written. While we come to many of the same conclusions, he focuses more on her failure and lack of power.

3. Weinstein also makes this point (5).

4. Doreen Fowler's excellent article, "Matricide and the Mother's Revenge," appeared while I was revising this chapter after presenting it at the California State Symposium on American Literature in May 1989. Fowler and I have independently reached many similar conclusions and employed similar methodology, relying on feminist revisions of Lacanian models and Margaret Homans's treat-

ment of the literal and figurative. But Fowler's treatment focuses more on the Lacanian move from the Imaginary to the Symbolic, while I emphasize creativity as an interplay between the physical and linguistic.

5. André Bleikasten, for example, ties Dewey Dell to the "Cosmic Mothers of mythology." She is equated with "mother-earth" as the "mysterious life forces that send tremors through her womb are no different from the ones that make the crops grow" (*Ink* 170–71).

Chapter 3

1. In contrast to the many condemnations of Temple's sexuality and, particularly, her perjury, a few sympathetic critics stand out. Joseph Urgo in "Temple Drake's Truthful Perjury," Dianne Luce Cox in "A Measure of Innocence," Elizabeth Muhlenfeld in "Bewildered Wilderness," and John Duvall in *Faulkner's Marginal Couple* all defend Temple's behavior, pointing out that while she may perjure herself in condemning Goodwin, he unquestionably has terrorized her and she may very well identify him as her chief threat, the man who instigated her ordeal.

2. Noel Polk, in "'The Dungeon Was Mother Herself,'" discusses Horace's identification with Temple after hearing her story. Polk suggests that Horace's reaction stems from a response to a repressed primal scene and represents a fulfillment of "his own rape fantasy" (73). While Horace "puts on" gender for reasons of self-punishment, Temple attempts to do so for self-protection. This comparison tellingly indicates the cultural definitions of gender: female as victim and male as protector. The novel, however, erases masculinity in that it presents all as victims in a world lacking protectors.

3. John Matthews, for example, asserts that "Ratliff is one of Faulkner's favorite characters, and his moral and literary brokerage in the Snopes trilogy resembles the novelist's own activity" (167). Panthea Reid Broughton, however, is more skeptical, suggesting that Ratliff's "final inadequacy as a Faulknerian hero is, I think, explained . . . by his chronic bachelorhood" (187).

Chapter 4

1. André Bleikasten in "In Praise of Helen" observes the way that "female characters have to be imaginatively reappropriated and reshaped according to the demands of male desire" (139). Yet he persists in reading Lena primarily as an earth-goddess, rather than elaborating on the implications of that reappropriation.

2. One noted exception is Michael Millgate, who calls their relationship "most important" and sees Lena as replacing Joanna by the end of the text (134). David Williams concurs with the notion of substitution, citing it as "a major part of the

mythos of *Light in August*" (160). However, I find Joanna so imaginatively compelling that I cannot accept the argument that Lena replaces her in any significant way.

3. For a fuller discussion of Joe's response to the combined threat of race and gender see Doreen Fowler, "Joe Christmas and 'Womanshenegro.'" Fowler argues that Joe's misogyny is really a form of self-hatred in response to his own feminine traits. See also Thadious Davis on *Light in August* in *Faulkner's Negro*.

Chapter 5

1. Rosa Coldfield gets most of the attention in these investigations. Linda Kauffman describes Rosa as a lover and embodiment of absence, while Patrick O'Donnell sees her as abject. For Minrose Gwin she is an uncanny hysteric, and Judith Wittenberg notes the way she both uses and rebels against patriarchal language. More recently, Linda Wagner-Martin has examined her as daughter, and Rosemary Coleman, very briefly, as mother. Leslie Haywood examines Judith Sutpen's resistence to the phallogocentric world of her father, while Jenny Jennings Foerst discusses the ways the women move into the erotic. Susan Donaldson notes that Clytie's silence stands in opposition to Sutpen's design, and Loren F. Schmidtberger meticulously documents the ways in which Clytie's knowledge should be perceived as real rather than mysterious.

2. Elisabeth S. Muhlenfeld, in an early article, points out some of the ways in which the supernatural is matched by a corresponding "real" presentation. Faulkner, she says, "painstakingly traces her movement toward 'ghost-ness' while, at the same time, emphasizing those aspects of her character which insure that she is never less than completely alive" ("Shadows" 291).

Works Cited

Abbott, Shirley. *Womenfolks: Growing Up Down South.* New York: Ticknor & Fields, 1983.

Adamowski, T. H. "'Meet Mrs. Bundren': As I Lay Dying—Gentility, Tact, and Psychoanalysis." *University of Toronto Quarterly* 49 (Spring 1980): 205–27.

Barnett, Louise K. "The Speech Community of *The Hamlet.*" *Centennial Review* 30 (Summer 1986): 400–414.

Bassett, John E. "*Sanctuary:* Personal Fantasies and Social Fictions." *South Carolina Review* 14 (Fall 1981): 73–82.

Benson, Jackson J. "Quentin Compson: Self-Portrait of a Young Artist's Emotions." *Twentieth Century Literature* 17 (1971): 143–59.

Bernhardt, Laurie A. "'Being Worthy Enough': The Tragedy of Charlotte Rittenmeyer." *Mississippi Quarterly* 39 (Summer 1986): 351–64.

Blake, Nancy. "Creation and Procreation: The Voice and the Name, or Biblical Intertextuality in *Absalom, Absalom!*" In *Intertextuality in Faulkner,* ed. Michael Gresset and Noel Polk. Jackson: University Press of Mississippi, 1985.

Bleikasten, André. *The Ink of Melancholy: Faulkner's Novels From "The Sound and the Fury" to "Light in August."* Bloomington: Indiana University Press, 1990.

———. "In Praise of Helen." In *Faulkner and Women: Faulkner and Yoknapatawpha, 1985,* ed. Doreen Fowler and Ann J. Abadie. Jackson: University Press of Mississippi, 1986.

———. "*Light in August:* The Closed Society and Its Subjects." In *New Essays on "Light in August,"* ed. Michael Millgate. New York: Cambridge University Press, 1987.

———. *The Most Splendid Failure: Faulkner's "The Sound and the Fury."* Bloomington: Indiana University Press, 1976.

Brooks, Cleanth. *William Faulkner: The Yoknapatawpha Country.* New Haven: Yale University Press, 1963.

Broughton, Panthea Reid. "Masculinity and Menfolk in *The Hamlet.*" *Mississippi Quarterly* 22 (Summer 1969): 181–89.

Butler, Judith. *Gender Trouble: Feminism and the Subversion of Identity*. New York: Routledge, 1990.

Chodorow, Nancy. *The Reproduction of Mothering: Psychoanalysis and the Sociology of Gender*. Berkeley: University of California Press, 1978.

Cixous, Hélène. "The Laugh of the Medusa." In *New French Feminisms*, ed. Elaine Marks & Isabelle de Courtivron. 1980. New York: Schocken Books, 1981.

Coleman, Rosemary. "Family Ties: Generating Narratives in *Absalom, Absalom!*" *Mississippi Quarterly* 41 (Summer 1988): 19–32.

Cox, Dianne Luce. "A Measure of Innocence: *Sanctuary's* Temple Drake." *Mississippi Quarterly* 39 (Summer 1986): 301–24.

Davis, Robert Con. "Critical Introduction: The Discourse of the Father." In *The Fictional Father: Lacanian Readings of the Text*, ed. Robert Con Davis. Amherst: University of Massachusetts Press, 1981.

Davis, Thadious. *Faulkner's Negro: Art and the Southern Context*. Baton Rouge: Louisiana State University Press, 1983.

Donaldson, Susan. "Subverting History: Women and Narrative in *Absalom, Absalom!*" *Southern Quarterly* 26 (Summer 1988): 19–32.

DuPlessis, Rachel Blau. *Writing Beyond the Ending: Narrative Strategies of Twentieth-Century Women Writers*. Bloomington: Indiana University Press, 1985.

Duvall, John N. *Faulkner's Marginal Couple: Invisible, Outlaw, and Unspeakable Communities*. Austin: University of Texas Press, 1990.

Eldred, Janet Carey. "Faulkner's Still Life: Art and Abortion in *The Wild Palms*." *Faulkner Journal* 4 (Fall 1988/Spring 1989): 139–58.

Faulkner, William. *Absalom, Absalom!* 1936. New York: Vintage, 1987.

———. *As I Lay Dying*. 1930. New York: Vintage, 1987.

———. *Faulkner in the University*. Ed. Frederick L. Gwynn and Joseph Blotner. eds. New York: Vintage, 1959.

———. *Flags in the Dust*. New York: Vintage, 1973.

———. *The Hamlet*. 1931. New York: Vintage, 1956.

———. "An Introduction to *The Sound and the Fury*." Ed. James B. Meriwether. *The Southern Review* 8 (1972): 705–10.

———. *Light in August*. 1932. New York: Vintage, 1990.

———. *Lion in the Garden*. Ed. James B. Meriwether and Michael Millgate. New York: Random House, 1968.

———. *Mosquitoes*. New York: Boni & Liveright, 1927.

———. *Sanctuary*. 1931. New York: Vintage, 1987.

———. *Sanctuary: The Original Text*. Ed. Noel Polk. New York: Random House, 1981.

———. *Selected Letters of William Faulkner*. Ed. Joseph Blotner. New York: Vintage, 1977.

————. *Soldiers' Pay.* New York: Liveright, 1951.

————. *The Sound and the Fury.* 1929. New York: Vintage, 1987.

————. *The Wild Palms.* New York: Vintage, 1939.

Feaster, John. "Faulkner's *Old Man:* A Psychoanalytic Approach." *Modern Fiction Studies* 13 (Spring 1967): 89–93.

Felman, Shoshana. "Rereading Femininity." *Yale French Studies* 62 (1981): 19–44.

Foerst, Jenny Jennings. "The Psychic Wholeness and Corrupt Text of Rosa Coldfield, 'Author and Victim Too!' of *Absalom, Absalom!*" *Faulkner Journal* 4 (Fall 1988/Spring 1989): 37–53.

Fowler, Doreen. "Joe Christmas and the 'Womanshenegro.'" In *Faulkner and Women: Faulkner and Yoknapatawpha, 1985,* ed. Doreen Fowler and Ann J. Abadie. Jackson: University Press of Mississippi, 1986.

————. "Matricide and the Mother's Revenge: *As I Lay Dying.*" *Faulkner Journal* 4 (Fall 1988/Spring 1989): 113–25.

————. "Measuring Faulkner's Tall Convict." *Studies in the Novel* 14 (Fall 1982): 280–84.

Freud, Sigmund. "The 'Uncanny.'" In *On Creativity and the Unconscious: Papers on the Psychology of Art, Literature, Love, Religion,* ed. Benjamin Nelson. New York: Harper & Row, 1958.

Geismar, Maxwell. "William Faulkner: The Negro and the Female." In *Writers in Crisis: The American Novel, 1925–1940.* 1947. New York: Dutton, 1971.

Gwin, Minrose C. *The Feminine and Faulkner: Reading (Beyond) Sexual Difference.* Knoxville: University of Tennessee Press, 1990.

Heywood, Leslie. "The Shattered Glass: The Blank Space of Being in *Absalom, Absalom!*" *Faulkner Journal* 3 (Spring 1988): 12–23.

Homans, Margaret. *Bearing the Word: Language and Female Experience in Nineteenth-Century Women's Writing.* Chicago: University of Chicago Press, 1986.

Irigaray, Luce. *This Sex Which Is Not One.* Trans. Catherine Porter. Ithaca: Cornell University Press, 1985.

Irwin, John T. *Doubling and Incest / Repetition and Revenge: A Speculative Reading of Faulkner.* Baltimore: Johns Hopkins University Press, 1975.

Jacobus, Mary. *Reading Woman: Essays in Feminist Criticism.* Ithaca: Cornell University Press, 1985.

Jardine, Alice. "Death Sentences: Writing Couples and Ideology." In *The Female Body in Western Culture: Contemporary Perspectives,* ed. Susan Rubin Suleiman. Cambridge: Harvard University Press, 1986.

Jehlen, Myra. *Class and Character in Faulkner's South.* New York: Columbia University Press, 1976.

Jenkins, Lee. *Faulkner and Black-White Relations: A Psychoanalytic Approach.* New York: Columbia University Press, 1981.

Johnson, Barbara. *A World of Difference.* Baltimore: Johns Hopkins University Press, 1987.

Johnson, Karen Ramsay. "Gender, Sexuality, and the Artist in Faulkner's Novels." *American Literature* 61 (March 1989): 1–15.

Jones, Anne Goodwyn. "'The Kotex Age': Women, Popular Culture, and *The Wild Palms.*" In *Faulkner and Popular Culture,* ed. Doreen Fowler and Ann J. Abadie. Jackson: University Press of Mississippi, 1990.

Kahn, Coppélia. "The Absent Mother in *King Lear.*" In *Rewriting the Renaissance,* ed. Margaret W. Ferguson et. al. Chicago: University of Chicago Press, 1986.

Kartiganer, Donald M. *The Fragile Thread: The Meaning of Form in Faulkner's Novels.* Amherst: University of Massachusetts Press, 1979.

Kauffman, Linda. "Devious Channels of Decorous Ordering: A Lover's Discourse in *Absalom, Absalom!*" *Modern Fiction Studies* 29 (Summer 1983): 183–200.

Kerr, Elizabeth. "The Women of Yoknapatawpha." *University of Mississippi Studies in English* 15 (1978): 83–100.

Kristeva, Julia. *The Kristeva Reader.* Ed. Toril Moi. New York: Columbia University Press, 1986.

———. *New French Feminisms.* Ed. Elaine Marks and Isabelle de Courtivron. Amherst: University of Massachusetts Press, 1980.

———. *Powers of Horror: An Essay on Abjection.* Trans. Leon S. Roudiez. New York: Columbia University Press, 1982.

Lilly, Paul R. Jr. "Caddy and Addie: Speakers of Faulkner's Impeccable Language." *Journal of Narrative Technique* 3 (1973): 170–80.

Matthews, John T. *The Play of Faulkner's Language.* Ithaca: Cornell University Press, 1982.

McHaney, Thomas L. *William Faulkner's "The Wild Palms": A Study.* Jackson: University Press of Mississippi, 1975.

Millgate, Michael. *The Achievement of William Faulkner.* Lincoln: University of Nebraska Press, 1963.

Minter, David. *William Faulkner: His Life and Work.* Baltimore: Johns Hopkins University Press, 1980.

Morrison, Toni. *Sula.* New York: New American Library, 1973.

Mortimer, Gail. *Faulkner's Rhetoric of Loss.* Austin: University of Texas Press, 1983.

———. "The Smooth, Suave Shape of Desire: Paradox in Faulknerian Imagery of Women." *Women's Studies* 13 (1986): 149–61.

Muhlenfeld, Elisabeth. "Bewildered Wilderness: Temple Drake in *Sanctuary. Faulkner Journal* 1 (Spring 1986): 43–55.

———. "Shadows With Substance and Ghosts Exhumed: The Women in *Absalom, Absalom! Mississippi Quarterly* 25 (Summer 1972): 289–304.

O'Donnell, Patrick. "Sub Rosa: Voice, Body, and History in *Absalom, Absalom!*" *College Literature* 16 (1989): 28–47.

Page, Sally R. *Faulkner's Women: Characterization and Meaning.* DeLand: Everett/Edwards, 1972.

Pierce, Constance. "Being, Knowing, and Saying in the 'Addie' Section of Faulkner's *As I Lay Dying.*" *Twentieth Century Literature* 26: 294–305.

Pitavy, François. *Faulkner's Light in August.* Rev. ed. Trans. Gillian E. Cook. Bloomington: Indiana University Press, 1973.

———. "Forgetting Jerusalem: An Ironical Chart for *The Wild Palms.*" In *Intertextuality in Faulkner,* ed. Michael Gresset and Noel Polk. Jackson: University Press of Mississippi, 1985.

Polk, Noel. "'The Dungeon Was Mother Herself': William Faulkner, 1927–1931." In *New Directions in Faulkner Studies,* ed. Doreen Fowler and Ann J. Abadie. Jackson: University Press of Mississippi, 1983.

Porter, Carolyn. *Seeing and Being: The Plight of the Participant Observer in Emerson, James, Adams, and Faulkner.* Middletown, Conn.: Wesleyan University Press, 1981.

Reed, Joseph W., Jr. *Faulkner's Narrative.* New Haven: Yale University Press, 1973.

Roberts, Diane. "Ravished Belles: Stories of Rape and Resistance in *Flags in the Dust* and *Sanctuary.*" *Faulkner Journal* 4 (Fall 1988/Spring 1989): 21–36.

Sass, Karen R. "Rejection of the Maternal and the Polarization of Gender in *The Hamlet.*" *Faulkner Journal* 4 (Fall 1988/Spring 1989): 127–38.

Schmidtberger, Loren F. "*Absalom, Absalom!:* What Clytie Knew." *Mississippi Quarterly* 35 (Summer 1982): 255–63.

Schwab, Gabriele. "The Multiple Lives of Addie Bundren's Dead Body: On William Faulkner's *As I Lay Dying.*" In *The Other Perspective in Gender and Culture: Rewriting Women and the Symbolic,* ed. Juliet Flower MacCannell. New York: Columbia University Press, 1990.

Snead, James A. *Figures of Division: William Faulkner's Major Novels.* New York: Methuen, 1986.

Spilka, Mark. "Quentin Compson's Universal Grief." *Contemporary Fiction* 11 (1970): 451–69.

Sprengnether, Madelon. *The Spectral Mother: Freud, Feminism, and Psychoanalysis.* Ithaca: Cornell University Press, 1990.

Stanton, Domna C. "Difference on Trial: A Critique of the Maternal Metaphor in Cixous, Irigaray, and Kristeva." In *The Poetics of Gender,* ed. Nancy Miller. New York: Columbia University Press, 1986.

Sundquist, Eric J. *Faulkner: The House Divided.* Baltimore: Johns Hopkins University Press, 1983.

Todorov, Tzvetan. *The Fantastic: A Structural Approach to a Literary Genre.* Trans. Richard Howard. Ithaca: Cornell University Press, 1975.

Trouard, Dawn. "Eula's Plot: An Irigararian Reading of Faulkner's Snopes Trilogy." *Mississippi Quarterly* 42 (1989): 281–97.

Urgo, Joseph. "Temple Drake's Truthful Perjury: Rethinking Faulkner's *Sanctuary.*" *American Literature* 55 (October 1983): 435–44.

Wadlington, Warwick. *Reading Faulknerian Tragedy.* Ithaca: Cornell University Press, 1987.

Wagner, Linda W. "Language and Act: Caddy Compson." *Southern Literary Journal* 14 (1982): 49–61.

Wagner-Martin, Linda. "Rosa Coldfield as Daughter: Another of Faulkner's Lost Children." *Studies in American Fiction* 19 (Spring 1991): 1–13.

Warren, Marsha. "Time, Space, and Semiotic Discourse in the Feminization/Disintegration of Quentin Compson." *Faulkner Journal* 4 (Fall 1988/Spring 1989): 99–111.

Weinstein, Philip M. " 'If I Could Say Mother': Construing the Unsayable about Faulknerian Maternity." In *Faulkner's Discourse: An International Symposium,* ed. Lothak Hönnighausen. Tubingen: Max Niemeyer Verlag, 1989.

Williams, David. *Faulkner's Women: The Myth and the Muse.* Montreal: McGill-Queens University Press, 1977.

Wittenberg, Judith Bryant. "Gender and Linguistic Strategies in *Absalom, Absalom!*" In *Faulkner's Discourse: An International Symposium,* ed. Lothak Hönnighausen. Tubingen: Max Niemeyer Verlag, 1989.

———. "The Women of *Light in August.*" In *New Essays on "Light in August,"* ed. Michael Millgate. New York: Cambridge University Press, 1987.

INDEX